THE SUDAN QUESTION

*The Dispute over
the Anglo-Egyptian Condominium
1884—1951*

by

MEKKI ABBAS

B.LITT. (OXON)

FREDERICK A. PRAEGER
New York

"BOOKS THAT MATTER"
Published in the United States
of America in 1952 by Frederick
A. Praeger, Inc., Publishers, 105
West 40th Street, New York 18,
N.Y.

EDITOR'S PREFACE

THIS series has so far been made up, with one exception, of books upon British colonies. The words 'colonial and comparative' which describe it were intended to suggest a new approach to the classification of dependent territories, but it is not easy to convey this with such brevity. The word 'colonial', except for historical usage, will soon be *in extremis*. This is not so much because the political relationship it defines is now widely condemned, sometimes with more emotion than knowledge, but because it is the deliberate intention of some colonial powers, one which Britain is well on the way towards fulfilling, to lead colonies into a new self-governing status. But at the same time that the 'colony', as a special constitutional relationship, may be coming to an end, it is being realized that the conditions of poverty, isolation and disunity which invited its establishment are by no means confined to those political units which carry this name, and will by no means automatically disappear from them when it is changed. It follows that within the large group of territories, which are now clumsily if tactfully called 'under-developed', there are many which, whatever their constitutional category, will gain from being studied alongside each other. And the process of disengagement from imperial control, both in its day and its morrow, is one that is full of interest. A series which contains the names of Ceylon and Ethiopia may, thus, for more than one reason, justifiably include the Anglo-Egyptian Sudan.

This country, for reasons given in these pages, was never a colony in name, but the title 'Condominium' meant little more than that it was a colony with two masters instead of one. The dualism itself, as Mr. Abbas explains, was mainly upon paper and in practice Britain has been the major and, since 1924, the sole power, administering the country. The student will therefore conclude for historical reasons what some Sudanese journalists have been quick to assert for the purpose of political condemnation, that in essentials the Sudan has been a colonial dependency and one administered in the main by Britain.

British Governments, however, have always been very correct in distinguishing its status from that of the colonies. This correctitude, as some Sudanese will admit, has not always been to their advantage and, in addition to all other difficulties and obscurities to which the Condominium status gave rise, must be added the veil which it drew between the British people and the country which, for all practical purposes, a British service was administering. It was nobody's business to press the Sudan upon the interest of a public and Parliament already hardly able to give proper attention to some fifty dependencies of less ambiguous status. On the contrary, the extreme delicacy of the Condominium compromise prompted a reticence which can at once be understood and regretted, and the Sudan, except at moments of open controversy between the two Co-domini, has been administered almost in silence. Of the few solid books dealing with its political affairs, the more important ones have been written by the British administrators who alone possessed the requisite knowledge, by Lord Cromer, General Wingate, Sir Harold MacMichael, men whose works are of classic eminence, and also by the official authors who have compiled more recent handbooks or descriptive statements. The present book, by contrast, is a contribution to the subject by an independent student. It deals with an outstanding question which, though now a major international issue, has not yet been set out in a full, up-to-date and scholarly form.

It is a personal as well as a professional satisfaction to be the editor of this book. Mr. Abbas and I share a friendship which began a good many years ago when he first worked with me at Oxford and which has continued both there and in the Sudan ever since. Furthermore, as I think I am right in saying, this is the first book to be published in English by a Sudanese author and this enhances my privilege in being associated with it.

The subject of the book differs a little in character from those others in the series which have dealt with government. It does not, for the most part, discuss a constitution so much as the diplomatic conflict that was waged about a constitution. But in the later chapters, with the entry upon the stage of the Sudanese as a third party, an inevitable and yet surprisingly unforeseen event, the actual character of the constitution which is to allow for their participation has become a major issue. We can read here of the rise of a nationalist group, or rather groups, demanding self-government, a story which provides interesting comparisons with similar movements in British dependencies, and no less instructive contrasts. The greatest of these are due to the existence of a double-headed sovereignty and the author shows how this has confused and even, in some measure, demoralized a movement which, in its colonial versions, has had to deal with a single ruling power.

In the events described in the later chapters of the book the writer played an active part, and it is therefore relevant to give some outline of his career. A Moslem Arab of the northern Sudan, born in a small village east of the Blue Nile, Mekki Abbas attended Gordon Memorial College and took up work under the Education Department. For many years he was on the staff of Bakht-er-Ruda, the Teachers Training College, which is one of the most vital and creative institutions in the Middle East. There he took a leading part in experiments in village adult education and in devising civic training for older pupils. Mr. Abbas became increasingly interested in mass, or fundamental education. When, in the middle thirties, the urban Sudanese began to stir into political life, he was at first prevented by his position as a government servant from joining them but when, in 1944, the nominated Advisory Council for the Northern Sudan was set up, he was made a member. He was also a member of the Sudan Administration Conference which in 1946 was set up to advise upon a new and more advanced constitution. He played a vigorous part in this and toured the country, including the south, in order to study the general situation. He resigned from the Advisory Council as he found membership incompatible with a new venture which he now undertook. This was the editing of an Arabic weekly newspaper of a political and literary character that was new to the Sudan except that, like all the others, it was strongly critical of the government. Between 1948 and 1951 he was in England, having been granted a special scholarship by the Rhodes Trust which enabled him, as a member of Brasenose College, to carry out the research which has resulted in the present book. He has now returned to the Sudan as a director upon the Sudan Gezira Board, which, on behalf of the Sudanese people, has taken over, from the two British companies, the control of the great Gezira irrigation scheme. In this position he holds a special responsibility for social development amongst the 25,000 tenants working on the scheme.

It will be understood that it is no easy task for students who come from countries which are in the ferment of what is, in the strict sense, a revolution, to deal with a subject which forms the very heart of the national issue in the mood of the historian and the student of politics. It is sometimes difficult for their academic advisers to know whether to agree with their strong desire to choose such subjects for their research. For this study the doubt seems to have been unjustified. There was a recent time when, in reaction from historical works too heavily stamped with the colour and pattern of the strong personalities who had written them, there was a tendency to exalt the opposite merely negative qualities of detachment and of the almost mechanical synthesis of exactitudes, the collection of which was an industry rather than an art. The impartiality we have, I think, more lately, come to value is that of a writer who does not attempt to sterilize his own character, but in pursuit of historical truth, encompasses his subject in the round and uses his imagination to interpret the actions of those whom, as a citizen, he might condemn or oppose. Especially noticeable in this book is the sense of justice with which Egyptian claims are set out in their full strength and legal validity.

It is true that the British reader will miss what may be the main theme which he probably connects with the Sudan, that of the great administrative achievement of his countrymen in a land which they found broken and depopulated, and which in fifty years has achieved such a high measure of order and prosperity that its leaders can now hopefully present a claim for nationhood and self-government. The first answer is the obvious one that the record of this administration is not the subject of this book. And if the reader still misses, in any incidental references to this record, the note of enthusiasm which he expected, there is an answer to this also, though a less patent one. It may be that history will confirm the laudatory assumption that run through many books by British authors upon British imperial achievements, but it is an inevitable, and perhaps a useful, counterweight that 'native' writers should regard the birth of political consciousness and assertion among the ruled as the more important and inspiring theme. The two attitudes of mind can be reconciled by those of both nations who understand that these movements, which for want of a more exact word we call national, are born of the union between, upon the one side, the British liberal tradition, expressed both in example and administrative action and, upon the other, of the political energy of a newly awakening people. Those who have been in countries where these movements are rising to their climax and have felt the political heat that they engender, will be best able to recognize the temperate atmosphere of the last chapters.

One of the most controversial issues, that of the relationship of the southern and northern Sudan, has been excluded from the body of the book because it played little or no part in the main diplomatic contest. Mr. Abbas has therefore relegated it to an appendix in which he has felt able to write more freely. I do not feel called upon, as editor, to offer my own judgment upon this question. I would only add that, while the author has said much in the appendix that seems to me just and true, he has not, perhaps, in this matter, been able to explain the strength or the character of the British view upon a most difficult problem, one which is of far too deep a character to be finally solved by any single constitutional decision.

This book goes to press while British troops, following the unilateral abrogation of the 1936 Treaty by Egypt, are in occupation of the Suez Canal zone, and while Sudanese parties are in feverish conflict among themselves and with one or other of the Co-domini, over the question of the political future of their country. With events thus in the melting pot they must, by the time this book is published, have assumed a very different shape from that described in its last pages. Any concluding words upon the subject I might write now are therefore likely to be inapt by the time they are read. I would merely record my own earnest hope that a most able and courageous people whom I have come to know a little through my friendship with Mekki Abbas and some of the other leading Sudanese, may be successfully helped by their administrators to escape from the dangerous and tangled heritage of the Condominium and to build a new, self-reliant nation-state which may live in amity with both the former Co-domini.

I should like to thank my research-assistant, Miss Chadwick Brooks, for the help she has given me in the editorial work for this book. This was especially heavy as the author was in the Sudan at the time of publication and he wishes to associate himself warmly with this acknowledgement.

MARGERY PERHAM.

Nuffield College, Oxford.
December, 1951.

ACKNOWLEDGMENTS

I am greatly indebted to Miss Margery Perham, the Senior Fellow of Nuffield College and also the Editor of the Series in which this book is included. But for the arrangements she made which enabled me to undertake two years of research work at Oxford, where she was appointed my supervisor, this book could not have been written. I have to thank her not only for her comment and criticism but also for undertaking, after my return to the Sudan, all the arrangements for publication. Should this book make any contribution towards a quick and just settlement of the Sudan problem, that country, too will be indebted to Miss Perham.

I have also to record my thanks to the Rhodes Trustees whose generous grant enabled me to carry out this piece of work.

In addition to my valued membership of Brasenose College, the Principal and Fellows of Nuffield College were kind enough to appoint me to a Studentship and I benefitted much from the seminars upon methods of research which I attended there. The College authorities were also kind enough to give me a grant to stay an extra term at Oxford to complete my work.

I am obliged to the Librarians of Rhodes House and the Public Record Office for the help which they so willingly rendered when I worked in their reading rooms. The Sudan Government Civil Secretary's Department in Khartoum and the Sudan Agent's Office in London were extremely helpful in providing me with information on a number of occasions.

I would also like to express my gratitude to Mr. A. H. Hourani, Sayed Abdel Magid Ahmed, Omer Effendi Mohammed Abdalla, Sirr el Khatim Effendi El Khalifa, Mr. A. Gaitskell, Mr. V. L. Griffiths, and other friends for reading the manuscript and making valuable suggestions.

CONTENTS

CONTENTS

PART IV. THE EFFECTS ON THE SUDAN

MAPS

ABBREVIATED REFERENCES

CROMER – Earl of Cromer, Modern Egypt, 2 vols., London, 1908.

HURST, BLACK & SIMAIKA – H. E. Hurst? Black and Y. Simaika, *The Future Conservation of the Nile*, Cairo, 1941.

ISSAWI – C. Issawi, *Egypt: An Economic and Social Analysis*, Oxford, 1947.

LANGER – W. L. Langer, *The Diplomacy of Imperialism*, 2 vols., New York, 1935.

LLOYD – Lord Lloyd, *Egypt Since Cromer*, 2 vols., London, 1933.

MACMICHAEL – Sir H. A. MacMichael, *The Anglo-Egyptian Sudan*, London, 1934.

S.C.R. – *Verbatim Records of the discussions of the* 175th, 176th, 179th, 182nd, 189th, 193rd, 198th, 200th, and 201st Meetings of the *Security Council of the United Nations*, 1947.

TOYNBEE – A. J. Toynbee, *Survey of International Affairs*, 1925, vol. I, Oxford, 1927–37.

F.O. – Foreign Office Archives at the Public Record Office.

ANNUAL REPORT – This reference includes the whole series of Annual Reports on the administration of the Sudan since 1893. The title was changed from Report by H.M. Agent and Consul-General on the finances, administration and conditions of Egypt and the Sudan, to Report by the Governor-General on the administration, finances and conditions of the Sudan, in 1912.

FOREIGN TRADE REPORT – Sudan Government, Department of Economics and Trade, *Foreign Trade Report*, Khartoum, 1947.

REVIEW OF COMMERCIAL CONDITIONS – H.M.S.O. *The Sudan Review of Commercial Conditions*, London, 1947.

SUDAN ASSEMBLY – Weekly digest of the *Proceedings of the First Legislative Assembly*, Khartoum, 1950.

INTRODUCTORY

THE COUNTRY AND THE PEOPLE

IT is not intended in this chapter to give a comprehensive geographical and ethnological survey of the Sudan. The purpose is to present, in general terms, those characteristics of the country and the people which will give the reader the necessary background to the Sudan dispute as it developed, first between Egypt and Britain, and later between these two and the Sudanese. Egypt claimed in the latest phase of the dispute that geographically, culturally and racially she and the Sudan were one and the same country, and therefore demanded that Britain should immediately withdraw and agree to a permanent unity of the Nile Valley under the Egyptian Crown, so that the inhabitants of the upper part of the valley could share the aspirations and prosperity of their more advanced brethren in the lower part. Britain took the position—and stood upon it firmly—that the Sudan was a separate country, and that its people had little or no racial affinities with the Egyptians but should be gradually trained in self-government and, when that stage was reached, should be allowed to choose for themselves the future status of their country. When the Sudanese appeared on the scene of this political controversy, they demanded the termination of the Anglo-Egyptian Condominium; some stood for independence, others wanted a Sudanese democratic government united with Egypt under the Egyptian Crown.

Which is right, Egypt, or Britain? Are their motives purely altruistic, or have they interests in the country to which they refrain from giving prominence in the debate, either because of a desire to win Sudanese confidence or because to base a case upon self interest is not compatible with the professed ideals of the United Nations? Are the Sudanese sufficiently qualified to manage their own affairs, and can their country support itself? These are the sort of questions which should be answered if the dispute is to be understood. It would be difficult to embark upon them until there has been recalled to the mind of the reader some picture, however slightly drawn, of the people whose welfare and future are at stake and of the country in which they live. An attempt will therefore be made in this chapter to deal generally with the geographical and ethnographical character of this region of Africa. The other aspects, such as the interests of Egypt and Britain, the education of the Sudanese and their fitness to govern their country, will be dealt with later in the book.

The Sudan is a vast country. It has an area of very nearly a million square miles, or a quarter of the area of Europe. It extends from the southern border of the temperate zone to three degrees north of the equator—a distance of about 1,300 miles. Its breadth from east to west is almost the same as its length, and within this huge area there are extreme differences in climate, soil, vegetation and ways of life. Its position immediately south of Egypt, its 500 miles of eastern frontiers facing Arabia across the Red Sea and its deep extension into the heart of Africa, are together responsible for the racial variety of its approximately eight million inhabitants.

In view of the striking ecological contrasts between the latitudes in this part of the world, the country and its people can best be presented in three zones—the north, the centre and the south.

The northern zone lies between the 22nd parallel of north latitude, which is the northern boundary, and roughly the 18th north parallel. A traveller by aeroplane in this part flies from Wadi Halfa in the north for more than two hundred miles over the Atmour desert, which is a continuation of the Great Sahara. As the air route does not follow the Nile which runs through the middle of this desert, the monotony of the sand and bare hills is not broken until the aeroplane reaches Karima and a thin green line of cultivation is seen with palm trees on either side of the silvery river. Except for the almost unbroken line of small villages along the banks of the Nile, and the scattered nomadic camel-owning tribes some 400 miles away along the Red Sea, no sign of human habitation can be seen.

Geographical conditions and modes of life along the river are almost identical with those of the southern part of Upper Egypt. These are; the lack of rainfall; the intensive agriculture on the narrow strips of land which have not been eaten up by the desert;

the extremes of winter and summer temperatures and the same square mud houses. The inhabitants are the most peaceful in the country. The magistrates of Wadi Halfa district may go for ten or twenty years without having to try a case of murder or of grievous bodily hurt. But much litigation goes on about land. A case about a fraction of an acre or two palm-trees may run into volumes and take years to decide. This is due to the scarcity of arable land which also causes a heavy migration of labour to Egypt or to the interior of the Sudan.

The more northern inhabitants of this part have close racial and linguistic affinities with the inhabitants of Upper Egypt who live between Aswan and Wadi Halfa. They are all generally known as the Barabra or Nubians. They are of medium build, not particularly muscular, and their skin varies from yellowish to chocolate brown. They claim Arab origins but historical and anthropological evidence shows that they are a mixture of Caucasians, who migrated to the Sudan in ancient Egyptian times, and the negroes who were the original inhabitants.[1] Their claim to be Arab is due in the first place to the infusion of a strain of Arab blood after the Arab conquest of Egypt, and its subsequent infiltration into the Sudan after the seventh century A.D. and, secondly, to the adoption of Islam in the whole region. Several Nubian languages of Hamitic origin are spoken but Arabic is the *lingua franca* and is the only written language.

Why, then, was the boundary between Egypt and the Sudan so drawn as to divide the Nubians into two halves? Wadi Halfa was considered to be the traditional boundary between Egypt and the Sudan. It was decided early in history by the difficulty of communications. Before Lord Kitchener built the railway which enabled him to transport his men and their supplies across the desert, travellers and traders had to choose between the river and the desert routes—two very ugly propositions. Caravans used to march either across the Atmour desert from Abu Hamad, or through the southern Sahara from Darfur is the west, to Assiut. They had to carry their food and water with them, and the six

[1] C. G. Seligman, *Some Aspects of the Hamitic Problem in the Anglo-Egyptian Sudan,* in the *Journal of Royal Anthropological Institute of Great Britain & Ireland,* Vol. XLIII, 1913, pp. 610–624.

weeks' journey was a terrible strain upon the men and took a
heavy toll of the 'ships of the desert'. The journey by river was
more strenuous if not impossible, because the great Nile, which is
considered by many modern Egyptian and Sudanese politicians
as Nature's proof of eternal unity, does not lend itself to navigation. There are between Wadi Halfa and Abu Hamad in this
northern part four groups of cataracts which render navigation
impracticable even for sailing boats. It is almost possible for a
man, when the river is low, to get across by jumping from rock to
rock. During the three months when the river is high the rocks are
not visible but they are so near the surface that even sailing boats
cannot go over the cataract area without running serious risks.
These were the reasons why Egypt, or any power that occupied it
and extended its political authority to the Sudan, found it difficult
to keep the country under proper control for long periods. The
construction of the railway brought the two countries nearer to
each other but Sudanese economic development and trade could
never have flourished had it not been for the construction of
a railway line across the eastern desert to Port Sudan on the
Red Sea.

Away from the river, in the Red Sea littoral, live the Beja
tribes—Kipling's fuzzy-wuzzies. The Bisharin and the Hadendowa, the two northern groups, are fine but fierce looking people.
They are warlike, reserved and resentful of outside interference.
One of their forces under Osman Digna during the Mahdist
revolution was the first to break through an English square with
inferior arms. They, too, claim Arab origins for the same reasons
as the Nubians but their features and their languages speak of
more Hamitic than Arab origins. The third main tribe is the Beni
Amer which lives in the southern part and extends into Eritrea.
The men are smaller in stature and more peaceful than the Bisharin and the Hadendowa. The Beni Amer, the hill Ababda of
Egypt and the predynastic Egyptians, are regarded by anthropologists as the purest representatives of the Caucasian Hamites.
But the mother tongue of the Beni Amer, strangely enough, is
Tigre which is a Semitic language.[1] All the Beja tribes are

[1] *Ibid.*, pp. 595–610. Also C. G. Seligman, *Pagan Tribes of the Nilotic Sudan*, London,
1932, p. 3.

Moslems and some of them are fanatic to the extreme. Here again, Arabic is the *lingua franca* and is the only written language.

Most of these peoples are camel-owning nomads and, with the exception of those who grow high quality cotton in the basin of Khor Baraka which rises in the highlands of Eritrea and gives out before it reaches the sea, and those who find employment in the docks of Port Sudan, they lead a rather precarious existence. The heavily eroded hills along the Red Sea are very barren, and the scanty rainfall, even when it is normal, is scarcely enough for growing the millet which is the staple food of the inhabitants. Revenue from the sale of camels in Upper Egypt helps the more northern tribesmen to augment the poor resources of their land.

Soon after the conquest of the Sudan, a number of British mining firms were given concessions to investigate and exploit any mineral resources they could discover. None of them succeeded in finding any mineral wealth of any appreciable size in the northern part of the Sudan. A rather poor quality coal was discovered in Dongola district along the Nile but there are, as far as is known, no geological indications of any workable deposits.[1] Gold was discovered in several places but the only workable deposit is a small one in Gebeit, west of Port Sudan. Aerial photographs indicate the existence of a small oil-field on the Red Sea coast but boring possibilities have not been fully investigated.

The central Sudan, which lies roughly between the 18th and 10th parallels of north latitudes is the most thickly populated and the most highly developed part of the country. Conditions of life along the river banks in this part, especially north of Khartoum, are in many ways similar to those prevailing in the north. The cultivable areas along the river are wider, but the population grow much the same crops. One notable difference is that the groves of palm trees, which are so characteristic of the north, gradually disappear as the traveller goes south towards Khartoum because the rainfall in this region destroys the date crops.

After flying for nearly 450 miles from Wadi Halfa, the traveller lands at Khartoum airport which is quickly becoming one of the busiest in Africa because it is the point where the Cape-to-Cairo

---

[1] S. C. Dunn, *Notes on the Mineral Deposits of the Anglo-Egyptian Sudan* (published by the Sudan Government), Khartoum, 1911, p. 7.

air line crosses the route from West to East Africa. The town is an irrigated garden city built on the tapering bit of land between the Blue and the White Niles which resembles the *khartoum*, or the trunk of the elephant. The older part of the town was laid out on the old site by Lord Kitchener who planned its streets on the pattern of the Union Jack. Between Gordon College in the east and the zoological gardens in the west are lined the main central government buildings. These with the Governor-General's palace, and the houses of senior government officials, run in a beautiful leafy avenue along the Blue Nile embankment. The business houses, banks, and residential quarters stretch south of the Blue Nile. The population of over 71,000 is a mixture of different nationalities. The cool dry winter of Khartoum attracts European and American tourists and visitors, but its dry heat in the summer, which reaches an average maximum of 109° in the shade, drives almost all the British officials away to England and brings the main activities of the government, and with them the political life of the country, almost to a standstill.

Opposite Khartoum, on the other bank of the Blue Nile, lies Khartoum North which is joined with Khartoum by the Blue Nile Bridge. It has a population of 34,000 who are mainly a mixture of Sudanese and Egyptians domiciled in the Sudan. Most of them are either engaged in the docks of the Sudan Steamers or are government officials working in Khartoum.

West of the main Nile, immediately after the junction of the two rivers, lies the great native city of Omdurman, which is by far the most interesting town in the country. Its population of 125,000 is composed mainly of the descendants of the friends and foes of the Khalifa who were concentrated during the last fifteen years of the nineteenth century in this *Bugatul Mubaraka*, or Blessed Spot, chosen by the Mahdi for the seat of his government. The friends were the generals, the congenial *ulema*, and the dervish warriors. The foes were those tribal leaders and religious heads who questioned the truth of the Mahdi's mission and who were brought for rigorous imprisonment or life internment before the Khalifa's eyes. The population is therefore almost a hundred per cent Sudanese and a visitor from any part of the northern Sudan can find some old relatives to accommodate him. Some of the notable features of Omdurman are the Khalifa's house, which is used as a museum of dervish armaments, banners, costumes, literature, etc.; a big open space in the centre, surrounded by long walls, where the Khalifa used to lead thousands of the *Ansar*[1] in prayers; and the splendid dome of the Mahdi's tomb, rebuilt in 1947, which towers over the houses, mosques and minarets of the town. The transfer of the seat of government to Khartoum did not deprive Omdurman of her leadership in religion, politics, literature, craftsmanship and sport. The Great Mosque is intended to be a miniature of Al Azhar for the spreading of Islamic teachings and culture; the Sudan Schools Club and other similar institutions have been, since the early days of the Condominium regime, the cradle of Sudanese literary and political movements; the bazaars are rich with gold, silver, ivory and leather handicrafts, and *Beit el Amana*—a wide space surrounded by huge stone walls which used to be one of the supply depots of the Khalifa—is the stadium to which thousands flock to watch with vociferous partisanship the matches of the Sudan Football Association.

These are the main towns of the Sudan. Other big towns are Atbara (38,000), the headquarters of the Sudan Railways, which lies just north of the junction of the Atbara River and the Nile 194 miles north of Khartoum; Port Sudan (47,000), the only sea port of the country through which the bulk of the trade goes; and Wad Medani (57,000), El Obeid (70,000), and Kassala (36,000), the provincial towns of the Blue Nile, Kordofan and Kassala Provinces.

South of Khartoum stretches the fertile plain of the Gezira, or mesopotamia, which lies between the Blue and the White Niles. About 25 miles south of the capital, our visitor, who was given such an unhospitable reception by the seemingly endless stretches of the lifeless northern desert, begins his jounrey through the million acres of green fields of cotton, millet and *lubia*, or hycinth bean. The cotton crop of this area, which averages about 40,000 tons of long staple Egyptian cotton lint, together with 80,000 tons of cotton seed with 24 per cent average oil content, brings prosperity to the local inhabitants, contributes over 50 per cent of the

---

[1] This term which originally meant the supporters of the Prophet was borrowed by the Mahdi for his followers.

government's revenue, and makes the trade of the whole country flourish. Indeed, should the civilizations which rose in the mesopotamia of Iraq and other parts of the Fertile Crescent have any future parallel in the Sudan, it will be mainly due to the prosperity contributed by this mesopotamia when its cultivable 2 million acres are fully developed.

The lessons learned from the agricultural development which took place in the Gezira in the first half of the twentieth century will be of value not only to the Sudan, but, indeed, to all the African territories which are not as yet economically exploited. In the realm of social and political ideologies the experience gained from it may well offer a valuable contribution towards solving the problem of the relationship of the individual to the community in the modern state. For these reasons, and because the Gezira Scheme is the backbone of the economy of the modern Sudan, it is hoped that the reader will be indulgent if a more detailed picture of this part of the country is painted.

The lessons which the Gezira provides for underdeveloped areas centre upon the problem of land and the tempo of expansion. Before the agricultural scheme was started in the Gezira the land was owned by the local inhabitants and, owing to the scanty rainfall which averaged 15 inches, the highest rent was two shillings per acre per year. When irrigation was introduced, first by pumping schemes and later by the construction of the Sennar dam, the government registered the land in the names of the original owners and compulsorily rented it, as it came under the scheme, at the highest pre-irrigation rates. The Government also restricted the sale of land to the local inhabitants of the area and to the state, and fixed the maximum number of acres which could be bought by any one individual. Then the land was divided into plots of 40 acres and these were allotted to the inhabitants as tenant cultivators. Original land-owners were given priority in the allotment of tenancies for themselves, their families and those who used to share cultivation with them on their lands, but no land-owner was allowed to have more than two tenancies in one name. This arrangement was generally accepted from the start because it recognized the title of ownership and paid a guaranteed rent which was considered fair since the landowners used neither initiative nor capital to build up the irrigation system which raised the productivity of the land. It is a middle course between expropriation and the full recognition of the liberties of the proprietors. Expropriation would have been regarded as a gross injustice by a people whose religion recognizes and respects private property, and might have caused serious trouble. Full freedom of the individual would have resulted either in the creation of landlordism, the dangers of which are too well known, or marred development on a wide scale as was the case in places like the Gold Coast.

The tempo of expansion in the Gezira is also well worth studying by other territories if they are to avoid the disastrous results of the East African groundnut scheme. When Lord Kitchener and his colleagues envisaged the development of the Gezira scheme in 1900 they did not follow the procedure of planning the whole enterprise on paper and approaching the British Treasury to guarantee a loan of some 15 million pounds immediately the plan was ready. They wisely began by starting small experiments with a view to testing the fertility of the soil, finding out the most suitable crops, how much water they needed and how they could best be grown. A solution to the problem of land had to be worked out, and research in plant breeding, pest control and soil chemistry to be started. While plans for carrying out these experiments were being executed, work was started on railway lines to connect the Gezira with the sea. When, by 1913, all the necessary preliminary work was done, a loan was raised and the construction of a dam across the Blue Nile was begun. But the work was interrupted by the first world war and the dam was not completed until 1925. This delay lengthened the period of experimentation and allowed the men working on the different sides of the project to gain fuller insight into the agricultural problems. When the dam was finished it was found necessary and wise to bring the land under the scheme, not all at once, but in instalments. This slow but sure tempo saved the Sudan from a serious sudden social upheaval and from the financial castastrophies which have befallen the East African groundnut scheme.

The lesson which may turn out to be useful to the world is related to the unique compromises the Gezira afforded between absolute state ownership and complete free enterprise, and between individualism and collectivism. The scheme was run, between 1925 and 1950, on a partnership basis between the Sudan Government, two British firms, and the local tenants. The Government provided the irrigation system and paid the rent of the land; the British firms contributed the management and undertook the supervision, ginning and marketing of cotton; the local inhabitants, as tenant cultivators, did all the agricultural processes and picked the cotton crop. There were over 21,000 such tenants holding tenancies of 40 acres each in 1949. The net proceeds of cotton were divided between the three partners—40 per cent went to the Sudan Government, 20 per cent to the British firms and 40 per cent to the tenants, each receiving a share commensurate with the yield of his plot. The tenants, in addition to their share in the price of cotton, which reached an average of about £200 in 1949, were allowed an area of ten acres each for growing their millet, vegetables and fodder. They took all these crops and paid no taxes and no rent for land or water.

The British firms ceased to be partners on 1st July, 1950, and the scheme became a joint partnership between the state and the people. The role of the firms in the new arrangement is played by a statutory corporate body called the Sudan Gezira Board.

This organization gave the state the necessary opportunity for developing the resources of the land for the benefit of the country as a whole without taking away the incentive to work which springs from personal interest. Yet the scheme has its collective features which are acceptable to the individual tenant and which have proved beneficial to the scheme as a whole. The expenditure on ploughing—deep ploughing in certain areas to eradicate some malignant types of grass—was a flat charge on all the tenants. The cost of fertilizing the poorer lands of unlucky tenants, and the charges of spraying cotton plants with D.D.T., sometimes from helicopter aeroplanes, to protect them against insects, were paid by all partners, the tenants share being born by them collectively irrespective of individual cotton yields. The tenants have a collective reserve fund for lean years, contribution towards which are made yearly by them, each according to his yield. Similar principles were insisted upon by the Sudan Government when individual Sudanese capitalists obtained licences to set up pumping schemes for growing cotton in other areas. How different could things have been in some Middle Eastern countries if such measures had been taken!

The conditions of life of those who are unable to draw upon the river in the central Sudan are determined by the amount of rainfall in the different belts. The region lying south of the Atmour desert and north of a line running roughly along the 15th north parallel, or just south of Khartoum, has an average rainfall of 1–12 inches—the southern parts have more rain and the average east of the river is higher than that west of it. This produces enough pasturage to render nomadic life possible for camel-owning tribes. South of this region, between the 15th and 13th parallels, lies a belt which has an average of 12–16 inches west of the White Nile and 12 to over 20 inches east of the Blue Nile. The part which stretches from the White Nile to the French Equatorial African frontier is mostly *goz* land, or vast stretches of undulating sand. The inhabitants grow varieties of millet, sesame, and groundnuts, and collect gum from the *hashab* or *acacia verek* trees. These agricultural opportunities make sedentary life possible and, except for the few who roam about with herds of sheep and goats, the inhabitants live in villages of straw huts. East of the White Nile, plains of black cotton soil stretch to the Abyssinian frontier. The people, excluding those who live in the Gezira irrigated area, lead much the same life as those who live west of the White Nile, but this eastern belt produces more millet and less gum and groundnuts.

The southernmost part of the central Sudan stretches roughly to the 10th north parallel. More abundant rains fall in this part and they produce richer grass, more acacia trees, and render more cultivation possible. The main occupation of the inhabitants is cattle breeding and they are therefore called the *baggara*, or cow-owners. About £300,000 worth of cattle were exported to Egypt, mainly from this area, in 1948. The export of cattle on the hoof may, however, be curtailed when the meat factories, which are being constructed by an English firm near Kosti on the White Nile, start to function in 1952. Besides cattle breeding, the *baggara* grow much the same crops as those grown in the region immediately to the north. They also grow, in the Nuba Mountains of Kordofan, a variety of short staple American cotton.

The geographical characteristics of the central Sudan, especially the more northern parts of it, are very similar to that of the semi-desert parts of the Arabian peninsula. So, when the Arab tribes migrated to the Sudan, either by way of Egypt after the seventh century A.D. or directly from Arabia across the Red Sea, they, like the earlier waves of the Hamitic Caucasians, drove Hamiti-cized negroid tribes further south and settled in the central Sudan, some in villages along the river, others preferring the tent life of the original home. So we find that the central Sudan, with some exceptions in Darfur, the Nuba Mountains and the upper Blue Nile where the inhabitants are predominantly of the old stock known as Sudani, is inhabited by Arab tribes. But even here the people's claim to have pure Arab blood is contested by historians and ethnographists. 'Everywhere they have intermarried with the indigenous population and even Arabs like the Kababish seem to have mixed freely with Caucasians speaking Hamitic languages and to a lesser extent with negroids.'[1] Erroneous interpretations by Arabs in the Sudan of the Islamic institutions of slavery and the acquisition of concubines led them to raid the negroid tribes of the south, capturing slaves and having as many concubines as a man could afford. These practices were, no doubt, responsible for the mixture of Arab and negroid blood.

The Arabic language is the mother tongue of all the Arab tribes and they are all Moslems. The Sudanic tribes speak their own languages and a form of Arabic and most of them have become Moslems.

The ethnographical and tribal divisions of the northern and central Sudan were, for the first time in modern history, weakened by the Mahdist revolution against the corrupt Turko-Egyptian rule. The revolution had a religious basis and the various tribes that rallied behind the banner of the Mahdi did so as fellow Moslems united in their *jihad* by a common cause. But as soon as

[1] J. A. de C. Hamilton, (ed.) *The Anglo-Egyptian Sudan from within*, London, 1935, p. 83. Note the chapter on 'Ethnological Survey of the Sudan' by E. E. Evans Pritchard.

the revolutionary years were over an oppressive system of administration under the Khalifa ensued and the common Islamic
brotherhood became weaker and weaker.

With the new organization of government, have come conditions favourable to greater unity. These include the building of
railways and the introduction of the motor-car, the telegraph
the telephone, the wireless and the aeroplane; the spreading of a
uniform type of education; the emergence of a Sudanese press,
and the introduction of semi-representative institutions of local
and central government. As a result the different peoples of the
northern and central Sudan are quickly being welded into a
nation bound together not so much by religious faith as by a
feeling of common citizenship.

The Egyptian claim that present day Egyptian and Sudanese
are racially and culturally one and the same people can only be
partially justified. The vast majority of the northern and central
Sudanese are, like the majority of Egyptians, Moslem in religion
and culture. There is also, in varying degrees, common Caucasian
and Arab blood. Nevertheless, there are differences between the
populations of Egypt and the northern and central Sudan which
make it difficult, if not impossible, to regard them as being as
homogeneous and as assimilated as the people of any unified
modern state. As regards language, the Arabic spoken by the
Kababish of northern Kordofan or the Baggara of Darfur or the
Shukria of Kassala is no nearer to Egyptian fellah Arabic than
that of Morocco or Hadramout. The usage and the intonation
are different, and so is the folk lore.

The whole physical and social environment is unlike that of
Egypt. These differences are due to geographical and ethnic
barriers. The bulk of the Arabs of the Sudan were, until the
improvement of the means of communication in the twentieth
century, cut off from the Arabic speaking people of Egypt by the
desert and by the Nubian tribes, who live along the Nile between
Aswan and Dongola, a distance of no less than 500 miles, and
whose mother tongue is not Arabic. Even racially the two types of
'Arab' are different. The Egyptian 'Arab' is a blend of ancient
Egyptian, Caucasian, Arab, Turk, Georgian, Albanian and many
other elements which were introduced into Egypt during the

numerous conquests which took place in its history. The Sudanese
'Arab' is a blend of Arab, negro, and some Caucasian elements.
The average Egyptian is nearer to the Mediterranean types than
to the Arabs of the Peninsula whereas the ordinary Sudanese is
nearer to the African. Dr. Taha Hussein goes as far as saying in
his 'Future of Culture in Egypt' that the Egyptians are by culture
and outlook more Mediterranean and European than Oriental
and Islamic.[1] The ordinary Sudanese knew no influence from the
Mediterranean nor, until relatively recent times, from Europe.

It is even more difficult to regard the Egyptians and the Sudanese as one nation since the peoples of the Sudan have only begun
to be formed into a nation in the twentieth century and since
there is no community of interests which in a modern state binds
peoples together. Both peoples are interested in the waters of the
Nile but this interest, as will be shown in Chapters VI and VII,
tends, in its present controversial form, to separate rather than
to unite them.

Finally we come to the southern Sudan. It stretches from the
10th parallel of north latitude to the southern frontiers of the
country which border on the Belgian Congo, Uganda and Kenya.
The rainfall, which ranges from 30 to 50 inches, makes this part of
the country vary from savannah to very nearly tropical forest.
It is, therefore, more interesting for the traveller to do the journey
across this part by Nile steamer than by air. From the roof of his
barge he gets a good view of the river and of the picturesque
country along its banks. The river north of Malakal, the provincial
town of Upper Nile province which lies north of the confluence
of the White Nile and the Sobat, is over a mile in width, and the
palm trees that grow along the banks in the far north are replaced
by tall grass and varieties of green acacia trees. The traveller sees
many varieties of birds, and, as he approaches Malakal, the sight
of 'yawning' crocodiles and grunting hippopotamuses becomes
quite common. He may see naked, black natives paddling away
in their dug-out canoes, fishing or hunting the hippopotamus.
The inhabitants along the river and away from it live in villages
of round grass huts with conical roofs similar to the villages of the
central Sudan. They breed cattle and grow millet and maize.

[1] Taha Hussein, *The Future of Culture in Egypt* (Arabic), Cairo, 1938, pp. 12–46.

South of Malakal the steamer enters the *sudd* area where the long thick papyrus grass, which grows in the vast marshes, used to block the course of the river. A narrow stream has been opened up for navigation ever since 1898, and the steamer, which, with barges tied in front and on the sides, looks like a huge raft, bumps against the tall grass as it is steered by its Nubian *reis* in the winding course at a speed not exceeding two miles an hour. Whenever it calls at the small stations it is met by crowds of tall naked, good looking tribesmen and women who emerge from the grass as the steamer drops anchor. These tribesmen are devoted cattle breeders and the cow plays an important part in their life and culture. Most of their clan traditions relate stories about cattle and many of their titles of honour are derived from names of cows and kraals.[1] Every new British District Commissioner is given the name of a bull which describes his physique and character. Cattle are also the medium through which they maintain relations with the spirits and the ghosts of their ancestors.[2] The other main occupations of the people are fishing, millet and maize cultivation.

This part of the southern Sudan is the home of tribes known to the anthropologist as the Nilotes. There are three chief groups of these—the Shilluk, the Dinka and the Nuer. Dinka land extends south into Bahr el Ghazal Province and some of the Nuer live across the border in Ethiopia. They are tall, long-headed, long-legged, dark skinned tribesmen. They are proud, conservative, warlike, and resentful of any foreign interference or influence. Although these three groups and other southern tribes are generally described as negroes, they are not so regarded by anthropologists. 'It is doubtful', Professor Evans Pritchard tells us, 'whether any peoples in the Sudan can be regarded as true negroes, and their non-negroid characters, their pastoral pursuits, and to a certain degree the structure of their languages, are attributed to to Hamitic admixture and influence'.[3] It is supposed that they are an admixture of early Caucasians and Negroes who were

[1] E. E. Evans Pritchard, *Economic Life of the Nuer*, in *Sudan Notes and Records*, Vol. XX, Part II, Khartoum, 1937.
[2] J. A. de. C. Hamilton, *op. cit.*, See E. E. Evans Pritchard, Ethnographical Survey of the Sudan, p. 88.
[3] *Ibid.*, p. 91.

later driven south by new waves of Hamites. Professor Seligman entertains no doubt that there is a foreign non-negroid element in the Shilluk and says that though this element is not so obvious in the Dinka and the Nuer there can be little question that it exists in them too.[1] He specifies this element as Hamitic Caucasian.[2] The Nilotes speak their own languages but a debased form or Arabic is the *lingua franca* not only here but throughout the southern Sudan. The majority of these and the other southern tribes are pagan though there are a certain number of Christians and Moslems.

When the *sudd* area is crossed the traveller, whether he goes south along the Bahr-el-Jebel to Juba, the provincial town of Equatoria, or west in Bahr-el-Ghazal to Wau, the headquarters of Bahr-el-Ghazal Province, passes through a country which is gradually changing from savannah into very nearly tropical forest teeming with big game. If he is lucky, he may see from the roof of the steamer in this area, or even while in the *sudd* region, a herd of elephants grazing in the tall grass. Other types of big game which live in this region are buffalo, rhino, giraffe, lion and many varieties of antelope.

While the two most southern provinces have so many varieties of wild animals, the number of cattle and other domestic animals is rather limited, and there are vast areas, especially in the west, where no domestic animals of any kind can be seen except the small dairy herds kept in government stations under special conditions. This is due to the tsetse fly with which these regions are infested. There are two varieties of this fly, one attacks domestic animals, with lethal effects, and the other attacks human beings and communicates the germs of sleeping sickness. The traveller in these districts sees, in places which have hospitals like Maridi and Yambio, long queues of inhabitants who come on special days for the inspection of sleeping sickness symptoms. The wild animals of this and the eastern area carry the diseases which are passed by both types of tsetse fly without being affected by them.[3]

[1] C. G. Seligman, *Some Aspects of the Hamitic Problem in the Anglo-Egyptian Sudan*, op. cit.

[2] C. G. Seligman, *Pagan Tribes of the Nilotic Sudan*, op. cit., p. 20.

[3] J. F. E. Bloss, *Tsetse Fly in the Sudan*, in *Sudan Notes and Records*, Vol. XXVI, Part I, Khartoum, 1945.

The inhabitants, who think that, when God was distributing animals to the southern tribes, they came too late, turned to the land for their livelihood. But, because of their primitive methods of agriculture and the poor soil in some parts, they were never able to have a standard of nutrition much higher than starvation level. The Sudan Government, therefore, devised, as a part of a wider development programme, an agricultural project whereby the Zande people, who live scattered in a forest area, could be settled in fertile spots where they could grow crops for their food and cotton for their clothing. The scheme is in its early years and there are agricultural as well as anthropological difficulties to be overcome.

Some large scale agricultural development is possible in a number of places in Equatoria Province. Experimental farms have shown that the soil and climate are favourable to the production of cotton, strains of upland rice, sugar cane, tobacco and tea.[1] But the chief stumbling block in the way of any development which aims at producing crops for export is the long distances which products have to travel before they reach the sea. There is timber production from the forests of the south but it is confined to areas lying within economic reach of navigable rivers.

The mineral wealth of the southern Sudan is worthy of mention. Surface deposits of iron ore exist in all three provinces and solid deposits are known to exist in Bahr-el-Ghazal and Upper Nile. The iron ores of Bahr-el-Ghazal cover an area of about 80,000 square kilometres and their thickness, which varies from one to five metres, may be much more in places.[2] Copper also exists in smaller quantities than iron in Bahr-el-Ghazal, and a workable deposit of gold is exploited on a small scale in Equatoria.[3] So far as is known with certainty, no coal of good quality exists in this or any other area of the Sudan. Deposits of good quality coal are known to exist in Ethiopia; those nearest to the Sudan are north of Lake Tana, near the Sudanese frontier post of Gallabat.[4] The absence of coal and the difficulty of communications are

---

[1] J. D. Tothill, *Agriculture in the Sudan*, Oxford, 1948, pp. 586–587. See F. Crowther, A Review of Experimental Work.

[2] S. C. Dunn, *op. cit.*, pp. 8–9.

[3] Sudan Government, *Sudan Almanac 1950*, p. 34.

[4] S. C. Dunn, *op. cit.*, p. 7.

2

presumably the main reasons for the absence of any plan to develop these mineral resources. The natives, however, have in the past smelted iron, using charcoal and clay furnaces. They used it for weapons, tools and ornaments, and the dowry in Zande land, up to the present day, is paid in iron spear heads instead of the payment in cows which is customary further north, where the tsetse fly does not prevent cattle breeding. The natives have also worked the deposits of copper in the past in the form of rings. The work was abandoned during the Mahdia.

Equatoria and Bahr-el-Ghazal provinces are inhabited by a variety of tribes. The two main groups in Equatoria are the Nilo-Hamites and the Zande, who are the chief of the ironstone plateau tribes. The Nilo-Hamites resemble the Nilotes of Upper Nile in stature but they differ from them in that their language and culture are more Hamitic. The chief Nilo-Hamites are the Bari. Professor Seligman draws attention to the occurrence of a type in Mongola Province, which is now called Equatoria, presenting certain Mongolian features. He describes the features, shows photographs of a Madi and a Bari bearing them and says, 'Whether description and photographs are successful in conveying a correct idea of the type or not, it certainly presents a definite and striking impression in the flesh. Nor is the type so rare and so little obvious as to be recognized only by a trained observer: we found plenty of laymen ready to make the pun "Mongalla is Mongolia" '.[1] There are also Bari-speaking types who are smaller in stature than the Bari and the Nilotes.

The Azande offer a sharp contrast to the Nilotes and Nilo-Hamites in physical appearance as well as in temperament and culture. They are medium-headed, and of medium stature, with a skin that may be described as copper-coloured. They are a cheerful, happy-go-lucky people, always joking and laughing, and are sociable and informative. They also have shown themselves adaptable to changing conditions of life. Bahr-el-Ghazal has a large number of Dinka and a number of smaller tribes of Sudanic origin.

Although Arabic culture has spread slowly but surely during the present administration, through the medium of political

[1] C. G. Seligman, *Pagan Tribes of the Nilotic Sudan, op. cit.*, p. 20.

officers and traders, geographical and political difficulties have stood in the way of a closer unification of the south and the northern parts. There are no railways in the south and the present means of communication is the Nile steamer which takes over a week from Kosti, on the railway line, to Juba in Equatoria. The journey to Wau in Bahr-el-Ghazal takes longer. Even this inadequate means of transportation was not possible on any regular time-table before the present administration started. Even the fact that both Malakal and Juba are on the air route to East and South Africa, coupled with the introduction of a Sudan Government air service to the south, have not brought the south much nearer to the north because travelling by air is far beyond the means of the ordinary Sudanese. Communications within the south itself are difficult and many places are not accessible during the long rainy season.

Political antagonism between southern pagan and northern Moslem originated from slave raiding and the slave trade which were carried on practically throughout the nineteenth century. The responsibility falls partly on northern slave hunters and dealers but mostly on the Pashas of Egypt and the Egyptian governors of the Sudan who permitted or encouraged these destructive enterprises.[1]

Slave raiding and the slave trade naturally created the strongest feelings of hatred against the northerners and against any foreign domination. So, when the Condominium regime began at the close of the nineteenth century, these practices were promptly stopped and every old slave in the northern parts of the Sudan could have obtained an emancipation certificate from his local District Commissioner if he had chosen to leave his master. The government also, in order to protect the southerners and to win their confidence, built up 'a protective barrier against northern merchants, which later crystallized into what is called "Southern Policy" '.[2] The southern provinces were made 'closed districts' to which no northerner was allowed access without a special permit, and were administered as a separate unit from the rest of the country. When the first step towards associating the Sudanese with the central government of their country was taken in

---

[1] See below pp. 27–29, 32.
[2] Sudan Government, *The Sudan, A Record of Progress*, 1947, p. 12.

1944, an advisory council was set up for the northern Sudan only. The deliberations of that council were restricted to the north and no questions referring to the south were permissible even if they were closely related to the funds voted from the revenue of the north for the economic development of the South.[1] This policy has for many years been the subject of much criticism by the politically conscious sections of the northern population who condemned it and suspected its ultimate purposes. These criticisms and suspicions were, however, partially allayed in 1948 when the Governor-General in Council, with the support of the British Government, passed the Executive Council and Legislative Assembly Ordinance which provided for the representation of the three southern provinces on the Legislative Assembly before which comes all legislation for the whole country.

A further important step towards the cultural unification of the north and south was taken by the Executive Council and Legislative Assembly in 1950. A decision was made to introduce the teaching of Arabic in all government schools and all private and mission schools above the elementary level. Southerners qualified for higher education started to go to Gordon Memorial College in Khartoum rather than to Makerere College in Uganda. These measures are calculated to promote a common outlook and a common feeling of citizenship.

Although the new orientation in the policy of the Sudan Government points towards a unified Sudan, the problem of the south still occupies the thoughts of some British officials in the Sudan, some men and women in England who take interest in Sudan affairs, and the missionary societies which have been working in the Sudan. For this reason the problem is discussed in some detail in Appendix 'C'. The reason for not discussing it in the body of the book is that it was never made an issue in the dispute between Britain and Egypt.

It is evident from the above account that the southern Sudanese who number two million, or one quarter of the total population of the country, have little or no racial or cultural relations with the inhabitants of Egypt.

---

[1] *Proceedings of the 4th Session of the Advisory Council For the Northern Sudan* 3rd–8th November, 1945, para. 4472.

The writer hopes that this brief description of the country and its people will give the necessary background to the dispute which will be presented and analysed in the coming chapters.

PART ONE

THE EARLY PHASES
OF THE DISPUTE

CHAPTER I

THE HISTORICAL BACKGROUND

BEFORE a survey of the dispute between Egypt and Great Britain is made, it is important to say a few words about Anglo-Egyptian relations generally and about the contacts of both Great Britain and Egypt with the Sudan before the dispute started.

British relations with Egypt first assumed importance in 1800 when the British Government, anxious to see Egypt free from French domination, helped the forces of the Sultan of Turkey to drive French troops out of the country. This action was followed in 1807 by the landing of a British force in Alexandria, simultaneously with sending a few British warships through the Dardanelles, as a warning to the Sultan against making an alliance with France. Later, in 1840, Britain, together with Austria, Prussia and Russia, signed a treaty with the Sultan to bring pressure to bear upon his vassal, Mohammed Ali Pasha, the Governor of Egypt, to give up his plans for overthrowing the Sultan by force of arms.

The year 1882 saw the beginning of the British connection with Egypt, which was to lead up to the dispute over the Sudan. In September of this year the British Government, having failed to secure the co-operation of France—then her partner in the Dual Control of Egypt—and of the Sultan of Turkey the sovereign of the territory, in suppressing a nationalist military revolt led by Arabi Pasha, landed a force in Egypt. This broke Arabi's resistence in the battle of Tel el Kebir and brought the country under British occupation. Although Britain's action was a fulfilment of a promise to the Khedive, given previously by Britain and France, to protect his authority, the aim was to safeguard her interests in the Suez Canal.[1] The Khedive retained his position under the British occupation and his cabinet continued to exist. But the

---

[1] Sir A. W. Ward and G. P. Gooch, *The Cambridge History of British Foreign Policy* Cambridge, 1923, Vol. III, pp. 136–137.

ultimate authority in important questions affecting the administration was assumed by the British Government through their Agent and Consul-General in Cairo who became the virtual ruler of the country. British authority, in consequence, was later extended to the direction of Egypt's policy in her southern dominion, the Sudan.

In dealing with Egyptian and British connections with the Sudan those of Egypt must be taken first, because Egypt, as a neighbour, has always had some connection with it. Egyptian dynasties in ancient history penetrated into the Nubian kingdom of the northern Sudan, and a Nubian dynasty once ruled over Egypt.[1] Later, whenever a foreign power conquered and administered Egypt—a process which went on from 525 B.C. when the Persians conquered it to A.D. 1882 when the British occupation took place—the political, cultural, economic and in some cases racial influence of that power penetrated, sometimes deeply, into the Sudan. But the event in Egyptian history which leads directly up to the dispute in question is the conquest in 1820 of the Sudan by Mohammed Ali Pasha, that great ambitious Anatolian, described by some historians as the son of an Albanian tobacconist, who came to Egypt with the Turkish expedition which expelled the French, and who later established himself ruler of Egypt under the Ottoman Sultan.

There were several motives behind Mohammed Ali's conquest: He wanted to reach the gold which he had heard existed in fabulous quantities in Sudanese mines; he was eager to find strong brave recruits for the new army he was building up for the execution of a programme of conquests that would take him to Constantinople, and make him Commander of the Faithful; he was anxious, because he had introduced the system of perennial irrigation in Egypt, to discover and secure the sources of the Nile; he was bent on developing trade relations; and he wanted to chase and exterminate the remnants of the Mamluks (Georgian Slaves) who fled to Dongola after the wholesale massacre which he had inflicted upon them in the Citadel in Cairo. The Mamluks ruled in Egypt before the advent of Mohammed Ali and he was afraid that they might remain strong rivals to his power.

[1] E. A. Wallis Budge, *The Egyptian Sudan*, London, 1907, Vol. II, Chapters I and II.

He sent an expedition under his son, Ismail, which defeated in battle the forces of the various disunited kingdoms and chieftainships of which the present Sudan consisted. The most important of these was the Fung Kingdom of Sennar, established in 1504. Ismail was later burned alive by the *Mek* (chief) of the Jaalin tribes in Shendi.

Mohammed Ali lost no time after the conquest in trying to get from the Sudan what he was after. Immediately after the occupation of Sennar, Ismail, accompanied by the French expert M. Cailliaud, proceeded to the mountain of Beni Shangoul, in the Kingdon of Fazoghli, above Sennar, in search of gold.[1] In 1837, Mohammed Ali sent a mission of seven German miners, headed by M. Resseger, a mineralogist, and escorted by five hundred men, to verify a report by the Egyptian Governor-General of the Sudan that gold mines had been found at a distance of 40 days march above Sennar.[2] He himself undertook a visit to the Sudan in 1839 at the age of seventy in spite of the hardship of travelling by boats and by camel. He went to Fazoghli to inspect the site of gold mines but he was disappointed to find that the quantities of gold were very limited.[3]

The recruitment of thousands of Sudanese youth for the Pasha's new army also started immediately. He 'instructed his son Ismail Pasha and his son-in-law, Al Daftardar, to send him as big a mass of Sudanese as they could muster. About 20,000 of these were sent to him and they were despatched to Beni Adi where their training started on modern military lines.'[4] Mohammed Ali was keen on recruiting Sudanese troops because he 'was reluctant in the initial stages to recruit Turks and Albanians for service in "Al Nizam Al Gadeed" (the Modern Army). These were by nature rebellious, disobedient and lacking discipline. Nor did he feel inclined to enrol the Egyptians as he feared the outbreak of disturbances in the country if he introduced a system of conscription to which the people had not been subjected by the Mamluk regime. He was afraid that conscription, added to

---

[1] Abdel Rahman El Rafi, *The Era of Mohamed Ali* (Arabic) Cairo, 1947, p. 138.
[2] British Consul-General Campbell to Viscount Palmerston: F.O. 78/319.
[3] E. A. Wallis Budge, *op. cit.*, p. 214, and Naum Shoucair, *History and Geography of the Sudan*, Cairo 1903, Vol. III, p. 25.
[4] Abdel Rahman El Rafi, *op. cit.*, p. 295.

the heavy burden of taxation, would be more than they could tolerate. Moreover, he considered that conscription of Egyptians would be detrimental to the supply of agricultural labour which was necessary if the country was to maintain good economic stability and become less exposed to financial hardships.'[1]

Mohammed Ali's other objectives were either partly or fully attained. Most of the remnants of the Mamluks in Dongola were the first to offer their allegiance and humbly to seek the pardon of the Pasha. Those who did not offer their allegiance fled south and finally disintegrated among the Arab tribes of the central Sudan. The attempts to discover the sources of the Nile were not as earnest as the search for gold. There were three expeditions led by an Egyptian army officer by the name of Selim Kobtan. He reached the *sudd* areas and sailed up the Sobat but never went further. The attempts to strengthen trade relations were not as successful as the Pasha had hoped. Gold deposits were disappointing, and the difficulties of communications, the backwardness of the people, and their primitive methods of production did not permit of prosperous trade relations. The only branch of trade which flourished was the trade in slaves. Slave hunts by the troops and private hunters were frequent and men, women and children were cruelly seized and many of them sent to Egypt.

Such were the aims of Mohammed Ali in conquering the Sudan, and there is no evidence, not even slight evidence, to support the allegations by present day politicians and political historians in Egypt that the sole aim of the Pasha was the 'Consolidation of the various parts of Egypt and the unification of its governmental institutions', because 'during decade after decade, during century after century, a solid background of common language, and common culture has been built up as the heritage of the peoples of the Valley of the Nile'.[2] We are also told that 'there has been no Egyptian conquest of the Sudan in the sense current in European history and usage. "Conquest" in the Islamic sense connotes a difference of faith, at least, between "conquerer" and "conquered". What happened was really a repetition of a phenomenon well-known to students of Islamic history, the

[1] *Ibid.*

[2] Prime Minister Nokrashy Pasha, S. C. R., 175th meeting, 5th August, 1947, Sections 35-38.

transfer of "power" from a multitude of holders large and small to a single holder more capable than the old ones of meeting new needs and of leading his peoples towards bigger ends. In answer, therefore, to the logic of the situation, Mohammed Ali built up one authority in one fatherland.'[1]

This presentation can neither be supported by evidence from Mohammed Ali's actions and the general behaviour of his officers in the Sudan nor by the previous history of the Nile Valley. The Pasha's craving for gold and recruits has been alluded to earlier. The attitude of his administrators may be illustrated by the contents of a letter No. 54 of 3rd Zilhedji, 1256 A.H. — 1839 A.D. from the Egyptian Governor-General of the Sudan to the Divan of the Pasha in Cairo. In this latter the Governor-General enquired whether he might be permitted to go into the Desert of Sudan 'to seize black savages, who were in their present state neither fit to serve God nor men, and to pick out from amongst those seized for the troops such as were fit to be made soldiers of, and sell away the others'.[2] This attitude is confirmed by the correspondence which went between the British Government and the Pasha of Egypt to which reference will be made later in this chapter when Britain's relations with the Sudan are discussed. The kingdoms which were defeated by Egyptian armies had long histories. The kingdom of Darfur was established in the fifteenth century and the kingdom of Sennar early in the sixteenth. Both these and other kingdoms were established on the ruins of older Sudanese kingdoms. At no time in modern history were Egypt and the Sudan politically united as one country. None of Egypt's successive conquerers actually ruled over the Sudan. Their political influence was confined to the northern Nubian parts and they had to be content with tributes which the northern Sudanese chieftainships agreed to pay annually.

But, although Mohammed Ali and his successors regarded the Sudan as a dominion, they were anxious to follow an enlightened policy in its administration. Mohammed Ali said in his address

---

[1] Dr. M. Shafik Ghorbal, The Building up of a Single Egyptian—Sudanese Fatherland, *The Unity of the Nile Valley and Its Geographical Bases and Its Manifestations in History,* published under the auspices of the Presidency of the Council of Ministers, Cairo, 1947, p. 61.

[2] F.O. 84/426.

to the notables of Sennar who were gathered to meet him, 'The people of other parts of the world were formerly savages; they have had instruction, and, by labour and perseverance, they have civilized themselves; you have heads and hands like them; do as they have done; you also will raise yourselves to the rank of men. You will acquire great riches and will taste enjoyments of which you can at present, from your profound ignorance, form no conception. Nothing is wanting for this purpose: you have a great quantity of land, cattle and wood: your population is numerous, the men strong and the women fruitful. Up to the present time you have had no guide: You have one now: It is I.' 'I will lead you to civilization and happiness.'[1] Said Pasha, the Khedive, visited the country in 1857 and showed much concern about the bad state of affairs which he saw.

It is to the type of administrative officer sent to the Sudan that the misgovernment of the sixty years of Egyptian rule can be mainly attributed. Many of the men in the administrative service were lacking in integrity and in imagination. Some were sent to the Sudan as a punishment for crimes committed in Egypt, others either because they were incompetent or generally undesirable. When they got there they made it their first objective to become rich.[2] They were corrupt and their system of taxation was too heavy. One of the slogans of the revolution against this regime was: *Ashara fi turba, wa la rial fi tulba* (ten in one grave rather than a single dollar in taxes).

So when Mohamed Ahmed Ibn Abdalla, the deeply religious son of a boat builder from Dongola, claimed to be *Al Mahdi Al Muntazar* or the Awaited Guide in the right path, he found in the malpractices of the administration, which were repugnant to religion, excellent fuel for his revolution. His religious faith, his magnetic personality and dynamic leadership, the people's grievances, and the general decay of the regime, enabled him in three years (1881–1884) of bloody revolution to defeat all the forces that could be mustered to suppress him, and to establish himself religious ruler of the country. He died a few months after the fall of Khartoum, leaving the country to be ruled by the

---

[1] T. F. Buxton: *The African Slave Trade and its Remedy*, London, 1840, p. 430.
[2] El Rafi, *Egypt and the Sudan, 1882-1892* (Arabic) Cairo, 1948, pp. 87–88.

Khalifa Abdullahi for thirteen years at the end of which the country came under the Anglo-Egyptian Condiminium.

Britain had no direct political or trade connection with the Sudan previous to her occupation of Egypt. To the British public, with the exception of those who read at the close of the eighteenth century, the travels of James Bruce in the Kingdom of Sennar and Nubia[1] and those of W. G. Browne in Darfur, the Sudan remained a part of darkest Africa. In the eighteenth century the British Governments were no less ignorant than the British public. Their lack of knowledge, let alone interest, is revealed in a report of the Committee of Trade and Plantations submitted in 1789. In preparing the part of this report on the state of trade in the interior parts of Africa, the Committee appealed to the British Consul-General in Alexandria for information. He wrote for them a memorandum based on 'frequent conversations with people, by some means acquainted' with the Sudanese kingdoms. On 'the condition, population, state of cultivation and government of those countries in the interior of Africa', about which he was specially asked to provide information, the Consul-General told the Committee: 'your Lordship's questions extended to matters not yet sufficiently in my possession to work upon, but I shall lose no time in obtaining them and of obeying your instructions to the best of my skill.'[2]

A little more information became available in the first half of the nineteenth century. J. L. Burckhardt published his travels in Nubia in 1819, and British travellers in Egypt began to collect information about the Sudan, and especially about the slave trade, from European traders and officials in the service of Mohammed Ali Pasha, the founder of the present ruling dynasty in Egypt. Following these reports, the British Governments and the British anti-slavery societies began, for the first time, to take active interest in the Sudan with a view to stopping slavery and the slave trade. In 1842 we find a very informative letter from the

[1] James Bruce. *Travels to discover the Source of the Nile*, London, 1790.
[2] Trade and Plantations Committee Report of 1789, Part VI. (Trade in the terior Parts of Africa.)

British Foreign Secretary, the Earl of Aberdeen, to the British Consul-General in Cairo, written on 2nd June. 'I regret to learn', he wrote 'by your despatch, No. 17 of 17th April last, that the conduct of the Pasha in respect of the abolition of slave trade is little in accordance with the assurances given by His Highness from time to time to your predecessor and yourself that he will put down as far as he can this barbarous traffic.

'I have to desire, that you will lose no opportunity of intimating to His Highness that Her Majesty's Government continue to look with interest upon his proceedings in this matter: and trust that they will be in accordance with the assurances which he has given to Her Majesty's Government'.[1] He wrote again on 6th July, 1843, 'I have to desire that you will seek an interview with His Highness the Pasha, and call his attention to the promise he made in December, 1837, to Colonel Campbell, that the practice of slave hunting should cease on the part of the troops; and that even if the abolition of all slave trade required sacrifices on his part, he would be ready to make them. You will remind him likewise of the declaration he repeated to you in July, 1842, that he would put an end to all slave hunts.

'You will express the deep regret of Her Majesty's Government at hearing, by the recent accounts from Egypt, that this barbarous practice still continues on the part of the Pasha's troops; and you will call upon His Highness to give effect and force to his repeated promises on this head by some public act, in order that the officers and agents of His Highness may be assured that it is His Highness' intention that, in accordance with his word, such cruelties shall cease.'[2]

The interest taken by private individuals and voluntary organizations in the suppression of slave trade began in the eighteen thirties and grew wider and wider until, by 1877, voluntary bodies were strong enough to influence the British Government. The leading individual who made representations to Mohammed Ali Pasha in 1837, Thomas Fowell Buxton tells us, was Sir John Bowring.[3] He visited Egypt on a commercial mission for the

---

[1] F.O. 48/426.

[2] *Slave Trade Papers*, quoted in *Reports of the British and Foreign Anti-Slavery Society*, 5th Annual Report p. 84.

[3] T. F. Buxton *op. cit.*, p. 428.

British Government and travelled as far south as Nubia. This visit gave him a chance to see what was going on and to make protests against it to the Pasha. Mohammed Ali himself referred to these representations when he wrote to the Governor-General of the Sudan in 1838 commanding him not to pay soldiers' arrears in slaves.[1] The pressure exerted by voluntary organizations is illustrated by a letter from The Earl of Derby, Secretary of State for Foreign Affairs, to the British Consul-General and Agent in Cairo on 29th March, 1877 in which he said, 'I transmit to you herewith copies of two memorials which have been addressed to me, one by a meeting of influential persons interested in the welfare of Central Africa, headed by the Archbishop of Canterbury; the other by the Anti-Slavery and Aborigines Protection Societies, praying that Her Majesty's Government will use their influence with the Egyptian Government to prevent the Khedive from extending his dominion over regions in Central Africa in the neighbourhood of the Lakes Victoria and Albert Nyanza, a proceeding which the memorials represent cannot be carried out without involving the Egyptians in hostilities with King Mtesa, and which they point out is, for the reasons set forth in their memorials, earnestly to be deprecated.'[2]

These purely humanitarian efforts, however, were frustrated by the procrastinations of the Pasha and the elusiveness of his officers in the Sudan but they were finally crowned on 4th August, 1877 with the signing of a convention between Great Britain and Egypt for the suppression of slavery and slave trade. The convention, which provided for the supervision of the Red Sea coasts and the inspection of ships by British warships, was remodelled in November, 1895.

During the second half of the nineteenth century British explorers, as a part of their scheme of African discovery, undertook the exploration of the sources of the White Nile. Speke and Grant entered Central Africa from the east coast to discover Lake Victoria. Having discovered it, they travelled north up the river and were met by Baker in 1863 near Gondokro in Equatoria Province of the southern Sudan. Baker came down from Khartoum and

---

[1] F.O. 84/426.
[2] F.O. 84/1472.

he, too, had the intention of discovering the sources of the White
Nile. Speke and Grant told Baker, after some reluctance, of the
existence of a lake to the south west, which they believed was
connected with the Nile system. Baker proceeded south and
eventually discovered the Albert Nyanza.

But the most important British contact with the Sudan before
the dispute started was established, not by the British Government,
but by individual British citizens. The two outstanding figures
were Sir Samuel Baker and General Gordon. Baker, as was mentioned above, first went as an explorer (1861–64). In 1869 he was
appointed Governor of Equatoria by the Khedive of Egypt.
Gordon succeeded Baker as Governor of Equatoria (1874–76)
and was later appointed Governor-General of the whole Sudan,
an office which he held from 1877 to 1879. Both men served the
Khedive loyally in suppressing the slave trade and in establishing
his rule in Equatoria. But while doing this they, like Rhodes,
Lugard and others in Africa and elsewhere, worked for the expansion of British influence. 'My chief endeavour', wrote Sir Samuel
Baker, 'was to work for the interest of Egypt, at the same time
that I sustained and advanced the influence of England. General
Gordon, who succeeded me, was actuated by the same desire, and
died in the hope that England would reach Khartoum.'[1] They
never succeeded, however, in bringing the Sudan under British
influence before Britain occupied Egypt, but both were destined
later to influence the British Government, Baker by his campaign
in the press and by personal contact with members of the Government, and Gordon by sacrificing his life.

With this brief historical survey which is intended to give the
reader the minimum background to the subject, we must go on to
consider in its different phases this dispute over the Sudan.

---

[1] T. Douglas Murray and A. Silva White, *Sir Samuel Baker, A. Memoir*, London, 1895,
p. 353.

CHAPTER II

THE ABANDONMENT OF THE SUDAN

December 1883—January 1884

THE Mahdist revolution in the Sudan was about a year old when the British occupation of Egypt took place. It was gaining momentum but the situation was not considered serious in Cairo, at least by the Khedive's ministers. The attitude of Sir Evelyn Baring, the British Agent and Consul-General, in which he was confirmed by the British Government, was to keep well informed about affairs in the Sudan but never to interfere with Egyptian policy. But the revolution took a serious turn in November, 1883 when the Mahdi's forces engaged and annihilated the Egyptian army under General Hicks at Sheikan, near El Obeid in Kordofan. General Hicks was a British officer in the service of the Khedive, and his army, which was despatched to suppress the Mahdi, was the strongest Egyptian force in the country.

The news caused a radical change in the British policy towards Egyptian affairs in the Sudan. This change of policy is the point at which the dispute began. The British Government made a recommendation to the ministers of the Khedive 'to come to an early decision to abandon all territories south of Assouan or at least of Wadi Halfa'.[1] When Cherif Pasha, the Egyptian Prime Minister, rejected this recommendation, he was told that he should either accept and carry out the British Government's advice or forfeit his office.[2] Cherif's government resigned and the British 'advice' was carried out by a different government.

When the British Government came to their decision on the abandonment of the Sudan they had before them a report by Sir Evelyn Baring on the military situation in that territory.[3] The

---

[1] Earl Granville to Sir E. Baring, 13th December, 1883, F.O. 78/3551.
[2] Earl Granville to Sir E. Baring, 4th January, 1884, Cromer, Vol. I, p. 382.
[3] Sir E. Baring to Earl Granville, 3rd December, 1883, F.O. 78/3560.

report included the views of the Consul-General as well as the views of the British military experts in Egypt and the Sudan. The opinion was clearly expressed in the report that it would be impossible for Egypt to hold Khartoum and the districts lying to the north of it as far as Wadi Halfa or thereabouts should the Mahdi decide to advance from the west. The opinion was based on the inferior quality of the Egyptian troops, their low morale, bad training and equipment, and on the difficulty of communications.

They also had before them the report of Colonel Stewart, who was sent to the Sudan in 1882 to investigate the situation.[1] Colonel Stewart's views on the military situation confirmed the views given in Baring's report. He also added, 'I am firmly convinced that the Egyptians are quite unfit in every way to undertake such a trust as the government of so vast a country with a view to its welfare, and that both for their own sake and that of the people they try to rule, it would be advisable to abandon large portions of it. The fact of their general incompetence to rule is so generally acknowledged that it is unnecessary to discuss the question.'[2]

In addition to these reports the heavy indebtedness of Egypt and her inability to finance a long war in the Sudan was taken into consideration.

The Egyptian refusal to accept the British Government's recommendation was based on arguments which Cherif Pasha stated in a *note verbale* which he addressed to Sir Evelyn Baring. The abandonment of the Sudan, he said, would cause a loss of prestige which was bound to weaken the authority of the Khedive in the areas where the inhabitants were either loyal or wavering in their loyalty: it would exercise a disquieting influence over the bedouin tribes which surrounded Egypt. Consequently Egypt would have to maintain a greater force for its own defence, especially on the southern frontier, where her best policy of defence had always been to maintain an attitude of offence against the hordes of central Africa to keep them at a distance from Egypt proper. He also added that if the Sudan were occupied and well administered it would serve as a suitable source of recruitment

[1] J. D. H. Stewart *Report on the Sudan*. Cmd. 3670, 1883.
[2] *Ibid*, p. 25.

for the Egyptian army and could be made to support a portion of the whole army of Egypt.[1]

Baring agreed that Cherif's argument regarding the security of Egypt was very forcible, but he was convinced that Egypt could not hold the country except on sufferance. Baring's alternative to holding the Sudan as a security measure was to recommend the occupation of Egypt, which was to be effected in a short time, to continue for a period of five to ten years after which Egypt would be expected to defend herself.[2]

No agreement was reached between Cherif and Baring and the Khedive had to appoint a new prime minister to carry out the policy of abandonment.

The British Government have been accused of forcing Egypt out of the Sudan so that they might annex it to their empire. Nokrashy Pasha said in the Security Council that 'the occupation of Egypt in 1882 gave the British the means for pushing their designs on the Sudan'.[3] The same charge is made by eminent Egyptians, writers and historians.[4] These charges cannot be proved. British pressure was brought to bear upon Egypt to evacuate the Sudan about a decade before the European powers, including Britain, began to seek spheres of influence in it. Britain had no strategic or trade interests in the Sudan. There is sufficient evidence to show that the British Government abstained from interference in Egyptian affairs in the Sudan until the situation became desperate. We find that up to early December, 1883, almost three years after the rising of the Mahdi, and over a year after the British occupation of Egypt, the British Agents in Cairo were instructed repeatedly by the Foreign Office not to interfere in Egyptian affairs in that territory. 'I need not remind you', wrote Earl Granville to Sir Edward Malet on 8th August, 1883, 'that Her Majesty's Government assume no responsibility whatever in regard to the conduct of affairs in the Sudan, and it is desirable that General Hicks should understand that although they are glad to receive information as to the progress of the

---

[1] Sir E. Baring to Earl Granville, 22nd December, 1883. F.O. 78/3560.
[2] Ibid.
[3] S. C. R., 175th Meeting (5th August, 1947), Section 38.
[4] El Rafi, *Egypt and the Sudan, op. cit.*, p. 101.

campaign, it is their policy to abstain as much as possible from
interference with the action of the Egyptian Government in that
quarter.'[1] The same attitude is reflected in Baring's report of
3rd December, 1883, where he said, 'I venture to express a hope
that Her Majesty's Government will adhere steadfastly to the
policy of non-interference in the affairs of the Sudan.'[2] It was not
until the Egyptian armies proved incompetent to deal with the
Mahdi that the British Government departed from their policy
of non-interference. Their sole aim was to stop the Egyptian
Government from 'increasing the burden on their revenue by
expenditure for operations which, even if successful, and this is
not possible, would be of doubtful advantage to Egypt.'[3]

Further, there is evidence to show that the British Government
were sympathetic with Egypt's efforts to suppress the Mahdi.
Sir Evelyn Baring and the British military chiefs in Cairo supported a suggestion by Cherif Pasha to apply to the Porte for
recruiting troops in Turkey[4] and the British Government agreed,
provided that the troops were paid by the Turkish Government
and that their employment was restricted to the Sudan.[5] The fact
that the British Government refused to send British or Indian
troops,[6] when Cherif Pasha intimated that he might request them
to do so,[7] goes to prove that at that time they had no designs on
the Sudan.

The British Government at this stage of the dispute cannot
even be accused of committing an error of judgment when they
predicted a victory for the Mahdi. Cherif Pasha's Government
considered that, even if their plan to secure 10,000 men, for whom
they proposed to ask the Ottoman Sultan, did not materialize,
they could, with their own resources, hold the Eastern Sudan and
the ports of the Red Sea and the valley of the Nile up to Khartoum.[8] Nokrashy Pasha and others[9] hold the view that Egypt

[1] F.O. 78/3551.
[2] F.O. 78/3560.
[3] Earl Granville to Sir E. Baring, 13th December, 1883, F.O. 78/3551.
[4] 1st December, 1883, F.O. 78/3560.
[5] 13th December, 1883, F.O. 78/3551.
[6] *Ibid.*
[7] 19th November, 1883, F.O. 78/3559.
[8] Cromer, Vol. I, p. 381.
[9] S. C. R., 175th meeting, section 38; also Dr. M. Shafik Ghorbal, *op. cit.*, p 66.

could have handled the situation with good results if the British had not interfered. But in view of the Mahdi's complete and repeated victories, which were rendered possible by a full-scale revolution against Egypt's oppressive rule; in view of the bad state of organization, training, equipment, provisions, communications and, above all, morale of the Egyptian armies, not to speak of the confused political and financial state of Egypt herself, it is not possible to give much weight to such Egyptian contentions. Later events showed that the defence of Egypt herself against attempts of invasion by Mahdist forces depended substantially on British military aid.[1]

This brief survey of the dispute in its earliest stage deals with the dispute between Egypt and Britain. But there was a third party about which a few words must be said. That was the Sultan of Turkey who was the ultimate sovereign of the territory. In fact Turkey remained in theory a party in the dispute until the signing of the Treaty of Lausanne in 1923, when she relinquished all her rights of sovereignty over Egypt and the Sudan.

The Sultan at this stage made no queries or protests either to the Khedive or to the British Government about the policy of withdrawal. The Turkish Ambassador in London, however, sounded Earl Granville on the possibility of the Sudan being taken over and held by the Sultan under his immediate sovereignty. When Earl Granville abstained from entering into a discussion of the subject it was dropped.[2]

This first phase of the dispute ended when Nubar Pasha, who succeeded Cherif Pasha as Prime Minister on 7th January, 1884, accepted the policy of abandonment.

1 Naum Shoucair: *op. cit.*, Vol. III, p. 520.
2 Earl Granville to Lord Dufferin, copy to Sir E. Baring, 11th December, 1883, F.O. 78/3505; also Lord Salisbury to the British Chargé d'affaires in Turkey, copy to Lord Cromer, 17th June, 1896, F.O. 141/315.

CHAPTER III

THE CONQUEST

1896—1898

THE second phase of the dispute did not open until 1896. In the meantime certain events, which introduced new elements in the dispute, had taken place.

The first event was the death of General Gordon, who was sent to the Sudan to carry out the policy of abandonment.[1] He was killed by the Mahdi's forces when they stormed Khartoum on the night of 25th January, 1885. Gordon's death left a deep impression on the mind of the British nation, and though the 'avenging of Gordon' was not one of the direct reasons for the decision to reconquer the Sudan thirteen years later, nevertheless it supplied a strong motive to the British soldier and was a source of satisfaction to the British public.[2]

Secondly, the European powers, in their scramble for Africa, annexed in the eighteen-eighties those parts of the old Egyptian Sudan which contained what are now known as Eritrea and the Somalilands. In the eighteen-nineties they competed for spheres of influence in the territories which make the present Anglo-Egyptian Sudan, which is the subject of the dispute. Britain made treaties with Italy (15th April, 1891),[3] Germany (15th November, 1893),[4] and the Congo State (12th May, 1894).[5] In all these treaties the Nile basin was evidently regarded by these powers as a British sphere of influence. Britain leased the Lado Enclave to King Leopold, and gave Italy the liberty 'to occupy Kassala and the adjoining country as far as Atbara', 'in case of being obliged to do so by the necessities of the military situation'. But at the

---

[1] General Gordon's mission later became a very controversial subject. See M. B. Allen, *Gordon and the Sudan*, London, 1931, Part III, pp. 199–419; and Cromer, Vol. I, Chapters XXI—XXVII.

[2] F. W. Fuller, *Egypt and the Hinterland*, London, 1903, p. 151.

[3] Sir E. Hertzlet, *The Map of Africa by Treaty*, London, 1909, Vol III, p. 949.

[4] *Ibid*, p. 914.

[5] *Ibid*, Vol. II, pp. 580–1.

same time Britain agreed with Leopold that the treaty 'did not ignore the claims of Turkey and Egypt in the basin of the Upper Nile'; and with Italy that the occupation of additional territory 'shall not abrogate the rights of the Egyptain Government'.

Thirdly, the development of irrigation works and the emergence of storage problems changed the Egyptian attitude towards the Sudan. They came to look upon controlling it not as a security measure but as one guaranteeing their water supply.[1]

Fourthly, came the accession in the same year of a new Khedive in Egypt, and of a Liberal Government in England. Abbas II was proclaimed Khedive on 16th December, 1892, at the age of seventeen years and six months. The youthful Khedive was the opposite of his father and soon proved himself an extreme nationalist and an anglophobe. He resented British interference in Egyptian affairs and dismissed anglophil ministers without that reference to the British Consul-General which was the custom during his father's reign. This attitude won him the admiration of the educated nationalists and revived the patriotism of Arabi Pasha's days. His first ten years of office saw a series of crises between him and Lord Cromer.[2] Later he yielded to British pressure only to revert to his earlier attitude soon after the declaration of the first World War. He was deposed on the 19th December, 1914. The coming of the Liberal Government to power in August, 1892 raised the hopes of Egyptian nationalists who thought that Liberal foreign policy aimed at effecting a prompt evacuation of Egypt and giving her her independence.[3]

These circumstances, to which may be added the intrigue of the representatives of France and Russia,[4] and of some anti-British Europeans[5] in Egypt, created a tense atmosphere which prevailed until the opening of the second phase of the dispute.

The decision of the British Government in March, 1896 to send an expeditionary force, composed of Egyptian and British troops, to Dongola, north of the great Nile bend in the northern Sudan, marked the opening of the second phase of the dispute. This

---

[1] See Part II, Chapter VII.

[2] Cromer, *Abbas II*, London, 1915, pp. 1-84; Abdel Rahman El Rafi, *Mustafa Kemal*, Cairo 1945, pp. 262-280; and *Mohamed Fareed*, Cairo, 1948, pp. 63-68.

[3] Cromer, *Abbas II*, op. cit., pp. 12-13.

[4] *Ibid*, pp. 9 and 25. [5] *Ibid*, p. 10.

decision aroused the opposition of Abbas II and of the Egyptian nationalists.

The policy of both Egypt and Great Britain, ever since the abandonment of the Sudan in 1885, was that the reconquest of the Sudan or parts of it should be effected as soon as Egyptian finances and military preparations rendered such reconquest possible.[1] Egypt was anxious to regain a lost dominion, and Britain was aware of her obligation to help Egypt to re-establish her authority over the territory she had lost, though through no fault of Britain, while she was under British occupation.[2] The question was considered in October, 1895 and the British Government advised that the reconquest should be deferred in favour of the construction of the Aswan dam which would help to improve Egyptian finances and enable Egypt to reconquer the Sudan without any financial embarrassment.

Why was it then that the British Government suddenly changed their attitude and decided on the reoccupation of Dongola in March, 1896, and why did the Egyptians oppose the expedition? The sudden change in the British attitude was due to a call for help from the Italians, who sustained a heavy defeat at the hands of the Ethiopians at Adua on 29th February, 1896. The Italians also received reports that the Dervishes were in league with the Ethiopians and that they were planning to attack Kassala, which was held by them. They therefore appealed to the British for a demonstration in the northern Sudan to divert the attention of the Dervishes.[3] So the British Government decided on the Dongola expedition. But although the relief of the Italians was the immediate aim of the expedition, British policy 'was in some degree the outcome of the rapid growth of the Imperialist spirit which about this time took place in England'.[4] The original British plan was not to advance beyond Merowe owing to financial considerations.[5] But later, when the Dervish resistance did not prove to be as formidable as had been expected, and when the French plans to force Britain out of Egypt by controlling the upper basin of the

[1] Cromer, Vol. II, p. 79.   [2] Ibid, p. 80.
[3] Foreign Secretary to Lord Cromer, 12th March, 1896, F.O. 78/4764.
[4] Cromer, Vol. II, p. 83.
[5] Foreign Secretary to Lord Cromer, 26th March, 1896, 31st July, 1896, and 5th October, 1896, F.O. 78/4764.

Nile became well known,[1] the conquest of the whole Sudan was decided upon.

The Khedive and the Egyptian nationalists opposed the expedition because it was conceived mainly in the interests of the Italians and because British troops were to take part in it.[2] They maintained their opposition throughout the campaigns and condemned the victories of an army, composed partly of Christians and partly of Moslems officered by Christians, over an entirely Moslem force. They even hoped that the Anglo-Egyptian army might undergo a defeat and some went as far as hoping that the Dervishes would occupy Cairo. Such men were not in fact moved by religious sentiment, but they were nationalists, anti-European in general and anti-British in particular, who wanted to appeal to the religious sentiments of the masses and to win support for their political campaigning. Abbas II gave these men his blessing because he felt strongly that Kitchener's victories constituted a British rather than an Egyptian gain.[3]

This time the dispute was not confined to Egypt and Britain. Turkey, abandoning the attitude of acquiescence she had shown in the first stage, intervened with some vigour at the beginning of the second phase. The first intervention was a query from the Grand Vizier to the Khedive with regard to the Dongola expedition. The Khedive was told in strong terms that he was not competent to send an Egyptian military force which was by the terms of the Imperial Firmans a part of the Imperial army, especially when such a force was going to act against Moslems. The message ended by saying 'It is impossible that this military expedition should be sanctioned by the Imperial Government.'[4]

[1] Sir Edward Grey's warning to France in Parliament (28th March, 1895), when a question was asked about the French secret expedition; also a note addressed by the British Ambassador in Paris to the French Government on 10th December, 1897, in which he adhered to the language used by Sir E. Grey in 1895, where it was said that the French advance 'would be an unfriendly act and would be so viewed by England.' The Marquess of Salisbury to Lord Cromer, 2nd August, 1898, F.O. 78/4955; also A. J. P. Taylor, *Prelude to Fashoda: The Question of the Upper Nile*, in *The English Historical Review*, Vol. LXV, No. 254, January, 1950.

[2] Lord Cromer to Earl Granville, 13th March, 1896, and 14th March, 1896; F.O. 78/4765.

[3] Lord Cromer to the Marquess of Salisbury, 12th April, 1898, F.O. 78/4956.

[4] Cromer to the Marquess of Salisbury, 31st March, 1896, Inclosure (1), F.O. 78/4761.

The Khedive, after consultation with Cromer, sent an answer which assured the Sultan that no encroachment on his rights was intended and that the object of the expedition was the same as the object of the forces that fought the Mahdi in 1883, to which His Imperial Majesty raised no objection. The Khedive also told the Sultan that the expedition was the result of agreement with the views and proposals of the English Government, which was in occupation of Egypt.[1]

This answer satisfied the Sultan,[2] but his satisfaction was only temporary. He resumed his protests in April, 1896. This time he protested against the landing of Indian troops at the Port of Suakin which was the port of the Sudan at that time. He told the Khedive to stop any encroachment on his rights in that port and informed him that in the event of his power being insufficient to stop any aggression Imperial troops would be despatched thither.[3] Several protests were also made by the Turkish Ambassador in London.[4] The British answer was to the effect that there was 'no intention of doing anything derogatory to the rights of the Sultan', and that, as the Indian troops were under the Sirdar, who was a servant of the Khedive, their presence did not constitute a landing of a foreign force. They also said that the presence of such troops was similar to British action in 1883 which was not opposed by the Sultan.[5] The British Government was determined, however, to stop, if necessary by force, any interference by the Sultan in the conduct of affairs in the Sudan. They gave the Khedive an assurance that they would protect him against any attempt by the Sultan to encroach on his rights and liberties granted by firman.[6] They also issued instructions to the Commander-in-Chief of the Mediterranean Squadron, when it was rumoured that a Turkish force was being despatched to Suakin, to stop such landing if it was attempted.[7]

[1] *Ibid.*, Inclosure (2).

[2] *Ibid.*, Inclosure (3).

[3] Cromer to Lord Salisbury, giving text of Sultan's telegram to Khedive, 24th April, 1896, F.O. 78/4762.

[4] Lord Salisbury to the British Ambassador in Turkey, copy to Lord Cromer, 3rd June, 1896, and 17th June, 1896, F.O. 141/315.

[5] *Ibid.*

[6] Foreign Secretary to Lord Cromer, 31st March, 1896, F.O. 78/4764.

[7] Foreign Secretary to Lord Cromer, 5th May, 1896, F.O. 78/4764.

These repeated protests of the Sultan during this phase were attributed in some degree to Russian intrigue.[1] But the assurances given by the British Government and the firm line they took about interference by the Sultan brought the Turkish opposition to an end.

Kitchener's expedition was a joint Anglo-Egyptian undertaking in which Egypt provided the title, the main body of the armies[2] and paid by far the greater share of the expenses.[3] Britain provided the leadership, a smaller part of the army, and all the funds necessary for the initial Dongola expedition.[4]

[1] Lord Salisbury to Lord Cromer, 17th June, 1896, F.O. 141/315.

[2] The strength of the Egyptian army in the battle of Omdurman was 17,600 officers and men. The British force totalled 8,200 (S. C. R., 179th Meeting, Section 42.)

[3] The total cost of the campaigns of 1896-8 was LE. 2,354,000 of which 1,200,000 was spent on railways and telegraphs, and LE.155,000 on gunboats. The 'Military expenditure' properly so called only amounted to LE.966,000.

Of the total sum of LE.2,354,000 rather less than LE.800,000 was paid by the British, and the balance of about LE. 1,544,000 was paid by the Egyptian Treasury.' (Cromer, Vol. II, pp. 105–6). (The Egyptian pound is equal to one pound sterling and sixpence).

[4] The money was first advanced to Egypt but the loan was later written off. (Lord Salisbury to Lord Cromer, 5th July, 1898, F.O. 78/4955).

CHAPTER IV

THE CONDOMINIUM

1899

AS soon as the destruction of the Khalifa's forces and the fall of Khartoum became imminent, the question of the British position *vis-à-vis* that of Egypt in the Sudan presented itself. It constituted the subject of the dispute in this phase and it has remained a live issue until the time of writing. Lord Cromer advised the British Government on the line of action to be followed in the event of the fall of the town and he was authorized to instruct Lord Kitchener to hoist the Union Jack and the Egyptian flag side by side at Khartoum, and to explain to the Khedive and his Ministers the significance of this procedure in these terms:—

'You will, however, explain to the Khedive and his Ministers that the procedure I have indicated is intended to emphasise the fact that Her Majesty's Government consider that they have a predominant voice in all matters connected with the Sudan, and that they expect that any advice which they may think fit to tender to the Egyptian Government in respect to Sudan affairs will be followed.'[1]

The British Government based their right to have this 'predominant voice in all matters connected with the Sudan' on the 'substantial military and financial co-operation which has recently been offered by Her Majesty's Government to the Government of the Khedive.'[2]

Lord Cromer turned over in his mind the possibility of making no special arrangement with regard to the political status of the Sudan further than the instructions issued to Lord Kitchener and his Ministers. 'I have carefully considered', he wrote to the Marquess of Salisbury, 'whether it would not be possible to allow

---

[1] The Marquess of Salisbury to Lord Cromer, 2nd August, 1898; F.O. 78/4955.
[2] *Ibid.*

matters to drift on and so settle each point of difficulty on its own merits as it comes up for solution.'[1] He thought that there was much to be said for this course if Lord Kitchener had to deal only with the Sudanese and with the problems of establishing a new system of government in their country. But numerous demands had been received from Europeans who wished to reside, to invest capital, and to acquire real property in the country. They could not be refused access, and the introduction of their capital was considered necessary for future development. It was, therefore, regarded essential and urgent by Cromer and the British Government that some distinct declaration should be made defining the political status of the Sudan.

It is important, before describing this declaration and examining it, to see what was occupying the mind of the man under whose direction it was drafted. Nationalists in Egypt, and later in the Sudan, said that his first preoccupation was the imperialistic interests of his country. Britain certainly had and has interests in the Sudan. But since British politicians and diplomats seldom stress their country's interests when arguing questions of imperial policy, it is not always easy to substantiate the imperialistic motive from their utterances. The question of British interests in the Sudan is, therefore, discussed in a separate chapter,[2] not in the light of what the British said but in the light of what has actually happened. But it would be unfair to say that because they have interests, whether professed or not, all their actions spring from purely selfish motives. There was certainly a great deal of sincerity and consideration for the interests of the people of the Sudan in Cromer's thoughts when he caused this declaration, known as the 1899 Agreement, to be drafted.

Cromer had had long experience in the problems of government in Egypt. He had lived and worked in the country before the British occupation, and, by the time the agreement was drafted, he had been for sixteen years the virtual ruler of that part of the Ottoman Empire. Egypt, demoralized by long periods of bad government and financial mismanagement, needed much

[1] Lord Cromer to the Marquess of Salisbury, 10th November, 1898; F.O. 78/4957.
[2] Par tII, Chapter IX.

reform. But there were many difficulties in the way of reform, chief of which was the long established European privilege in the Turkish dominions. Egypt was more burdened with European privileges, known as the capitulations, than any other part of the Sultan's domains. The reason was that the Khedive Ismail freely granted commercial and other privileges under the pressure of financial difficulties. Before any European could be punished for a crime he must be proved to have committed an offence, not against Egyptian laws but against the laws of his own country. Egyptian courts had no jurisdiction over Europeans. 'There were no fewer than seventeen Consular Tribunals, and in most of them the merest travesty of justice was administered. Europeans were systematically acquitted of crimes and offences which there was no difficulty in proving, while it was difficult for natives to come by their rights when the aggressors were aliens. Moreover these exotic jurisdictions had gradually been extended in directions never intended originally.'[1] European smugglers carried on their illicit trade under the eyes of the Egyptian Customs Authorities because treaty engagements forbade any prompt and effective action being taken against them. 'Those engagements have also been turned to such base uses that they have protected the keeper of the gambling-hell, the vendor of adulterated drinks, the receiver of stolen goods, and the careless apothecary who supplies his customer with poison in the place of some healing drugs.'[2] The house tax and the professional tax were not paid by Europeans. 'The reason why they did not pay them was because they did not like paying them.'[3] The European Powers insisted on the retention of these privileges, especially because their abolition or modification was coming from Britain, whose occupation of Egypt they had opposed.

Now Europeans were demanding to go to the Sudan which, for the sixty years previous to the Madhist revolution, had been a part of the Ottoman Empire. Should they, Cromer asked, be admitted under the same terms? It was 'manifestly absurd that British lives should be sacrificed and British treasure expended

---

[1] Sir. A. W. Ward and G. P. Gooch, *op. cit.*, Vol. III, p. 164.
[2] Cromer, Vol. II, p. 428.
[3] *Ibid.*, p. 435.

merely in order to place additional arms in the hands of Powers, some one or other of whom might at some future time become the enemy of England.'[1] Were the finances of the Sudan, when that country should become capable of producing revenue, going to be controlled by the Commissioners of the Debt? Cromer's answer was an emphatic negative. Under what conditions then could the Europeans and their capital be admitted into the Sudan?

According to the familiar procedure of international law, Cromer thought, the Sudan could either be returned to the Sultan and the Khedive as a former dominion, or be annexed to the British Empire. The first solution would satisfy Egypt and Turkey and the European Powers, especially France who was compelled to withdraw from Fashoda because Britain was restoring the authority of the Khedive. But, in addition to depriving Britain of the claims accruing to her by her participation in the conquest, such a course would perpetuate European privilege in the Sudan. The second solution would satisfy British claims and would save the Sudan from the capitulations but would be unjust to Egypt and would create political difficulties with France. 'It was, therefore, necessary to invent some method by which the Sudan should be, at one and the same time, Egyptian to such an extent as to satisfy equitable and political exigencies, and yet sufficiently British to prevent the adminstration of the country from being hampered by the international burr which necessarily hung on to the skirts of Egyptian political existence.'[2]

The method invented, was, to use Cromer's words, a 'hybrid' form of government, hitherto unknown to international jurisprudence. The instrument creating this new form of government was the 1899 Agreement,[3] generally known as the Condominium Agreement which has been, ever since its signature on 19th January, 1899, by Lord Cromer and the Egyptian Foreign Minister, the constitutional charter of the Sudan.

Lord Cromer, in forwarding the proposals for this agreement to the Marquess of Salisbury, submitted a memorandum

[1] Cromer, Vol. II, p. 114.
[2] *Ibid.*, pp. 114-115.
[3] For full text see Appendix 'A'.

4

containing his arguments for the principles followed and for the inclusion of each article.[1] This important memorandum is given in Appendix 'B'. It is, therefore, only necessary here to give a brief survey of the Agreement.

One of the main features of the Agreement is the denunciation of the system of capitulations running through ten of its twelve articles. The last two articles prohibit the exportation and importation of slaves, and provide that special attention shall be paid to the Brussels Act of 2nd July, 1890, in respect to the import, sale and manufacture of firearms and ammunitions, and distilled or spirituous liquors.

The title of the Agreement is: Agreement between Her Britannic Majesty's Government and the Government of His Highness the Khedive of Egypt, relative to the future administration of the Sudan. This was so very carefully drafted as, in the first place, to leave the question of sovereignty in suspense, and, in the second place, not to appear contradictory to the Sultan's firman to the Khedive which laid down that he 'shall not on any pretext or motive, abandon to others, in whole or in part, the privileges accorded to Egypt, which are intrusted to him, and which pertain to the inherent rights of the Sovereign Power, nor any portion of the territory.'

The preamble alludes to the rights of the Khedive incidentally and inferentially by saying, 'Whereas certain provinces in the Sudan which were rebelling against the authority of His Highness have now been re-conquered', while the rights of Britain are given prominence thus: 'and whereas it is desired to give effect to the claims which have accrued to Her Britannic Majesty's Government, by right of conquest, to share in the present settlement and future working and development of the said system of administration and legislation.'

On this drafting Cromer says, 'It appears necessary to state these rights as they alone constitute the real justification for the creation of a political and administrative status in the Sudan different to that which exists in Egypt'.[2]

Article I defines the boundaries of the Sudan.

---

[1] Lord Cromer to the Marquess of Salisbury, 20th November, 1898. F.O. 78/4957.
[2] *Ibid.*

Article II lays down that the British and Egyptian flags shall be used together.

Articles, III, IV and V vest the supreme military and civil authority in one officer, the Governor-General, who is to be responsible for making, altering or abrogating by proclamation all the laws, orders and regulations with the full force of law. No Egyptian law, decree, or ministerial *arrêté* is allowed to apply to the Sudan 'save in so far as the name shall be applied by proclamation of the Governor-General'. The Governor-General 'shall be appointed by Khedival Decree on the recommendation of Her Britannic Majesty's Government, and shall be removed by Khedival Decree, with the consent of Her Britannic Majesty's Government'. This procedure was borrowed from that of the appointment of the Commissioners of the Debt. It is needless to say how much better this arrangement is than that of appointing two governors-general, each to represent his own government, as in the Condominium of the New Hebrides. The Governor-General was given a free hand in legislation since he was only required to *notify* the British Agent and Consul-General in Cairo and the Egyptian Prime Minister of the laws made.

Article VI lays down that 'no special privileges shall be accorded to the subjects of any one or more Power'.

Article VII regulates the import and export duties. It gave the Sudan a separate commercial regime.

Article VIII put the Sudan outside the jurisdiction of the Mixed Tribunals.

Article IX put the country temporarily under martial law, and Article X excluded Consuls, Vice-Consuls, or Consular Agents from being accredited in respect of the Sudan without the previous consent of the British Government.

As soon as the Agreement was signed, Lord Kitchener, who was Sirdar, or Commander-in-Chief of the Egyptian army, was appointed Governor-General of the Sudan also. All the high posts in the administration were given to British officers. The highest posts given to the Egyptians, leaving aside the posts in the Mohammedan law courts which were naturally filled by them, were those of 'mamurs', which were subordinate to those of assistant district commissioners. Egypt had to meet the deficit in the early years,[1] and she paid an annuity of one million pounds which represented five-sixths of the joint military expenditure in the country.

Egyptian feeling against the Agreement was rather strong and Botrus Ghali Pasha, the Foreign Minister who signed it with Lord Cromer, was later assassinated. The abolition of European privilege as an argument for having a separate regime in the Sudan did not weigh very much with the Khedive and Egyptian nationalists, who had, as we have seen, always suspected that the reconquest of the Sudan would benefit Britain rather than Egypt. Even if they accepted the argument they could not accept the status of a junior partner in the Condominium. They felt, and justification for their feeling can be found in Cromer's arguments,[2] that Britain might not have accepted them as a partner if the Sudan was not a financial liability. So, in view of their greater expenditure in men and money during the campaigns, and because of the cost of the Sudan after the conquest, and because they found themselves a junior partner, they felt much aggrieved. The British argument for assuming the major responsibility was that Egypt could never have been able to conquer the Sudan but for the leadership of Lord Kitchener and his officers, and for the financial contribution made by the British Treasury for the initial Dongola expedition when the Commissioners of the Debt refused to approve the expenditure of the LE.500,000 voted by the Egyptian Government. When two people become partners in a concern it is difficult to assess the value of such a thing as leadership. But if the contributions in men and money were to be the only criterion the Egyptian grievances were justified. But Egypt herself was under British occupation and her own affairs were being managed by British administrators. Her subordination to the British in the Sudan was, therefore, an extension of the same subordination which had been imposed upon her government at home.

Although the second phase of the dispute ended with the launching of the new administrative regime in the Sudan, yet the question of sovereignty over the Sudan and the legal validity of the 1899 Agreement continued to be an issue in all subsequent

---

[1] Egypt balanced Sudan budget from 1899 to 1912, MacMichael, p. 240.
[2] Appendix 'B'.

phases. It is, therefore, necessary to discuss these aspects of the Agreement.

The history of sovereignty over the Sudan is so complicated and so anomalous that an attempt must be made to trace it before the situations which arose in the subsequent phases, and especially in the latest phase, are considered. It was mentioned earlier that before Mohammed Ali Pasha conquered the territories lying south of Egypt in 1820, the Sudan with its present boundaries did not exist. What existed were the Kingdoms of Nubia, Sennar, and Darfur. South of these lay districts inhabited by various tribes, each ruled by its own chief. None of the kings and chiefs knew or was known to the world. The whole area, according to international law, was *res nullius*.

When Mohammed Ali conquered these districts he did so in the name of his suzerain, the Ottoman Sultan, whose permission he had secured before he embarked on the conquest.[1] When his son Ismail, who commanded the expedition, arrived at Sennar, he made the notables swear allegiance to the Sultan.[2] The territories came to be known as the 'Egyptian Sudan' and were brought under Turkish sovereignty. In 1841 the Sultan issued a firman conferring on Mohammed Ali the governorship of the Sudan for his life. Later firmans recognized the rulers of Egypt descending from him as rulers of the Sudan also. But those firmans laid down that the Khedive of Egypt 'shall not, on any pretext or motive, abandon to others, in whole or in part, the privileges accorded to Egypt, which are intrusted to him, and which pertain to the inherent rights of the Sovereign Power, nor any portion of the territory.'[3]

This arrangement lasted until Egypt, at the behest of Britain abandoned the Sudan in 1884. From this date until the Anglo-Egyptian Conquest of 1898, the Mahdi and his successor managed to destroy completely any Egyptian or Turkish authority. What, then, was the status of the country in this period? Did the Sudan become *res nullius* because the period was long enough to extinguish all Turkish sovereignty, or was the Sudan a part of the Turkish Empire temporarily occupied by a rebellious army, or did it

[1] Dr. M. F. Shukry, *Egypt and Sovereignty over the Sudan* (Arabic), Cairo, 1946, p. 5.

[2] *Ibid.*, p. 5.

[3] Cromer to Lord Salisbury, 10th November, 1898, F.O. 78/4957.

become an independent sovereign state? No judgment was passed on the subject by any international court, but in the field of diplomacy the Sudan was sometimes regarded as *res nullius* and sometimes as a territory over which the Khedive and the Sultan continued to maintain sovereign rights. When Great Britain leased parts of it to King Leopold and allowed Italy to occupy Kassala and a stretch of land beyond it, without the concurrence or even the knowledge of the Khedive and the Sultan, she evidently regarded it as *res nullius*.[1] During this time France questioned Britain's action on the grounds that the latter was encroaching on the rights of Egypt and Turkey.[2] Later, when France sent a secret expedition to the Upper Nile, France and Britain exchanged places. When the Sultan protested against the Dongola expedition and against the landing of British and Indian troops at Suakin, he was assured by Britain and the Khedive that the aim of the expedition was similar to that of expeditions previously sent to fight the Mahdi, and that the landing of British and Indian troops constituted no encroachment on his rights because those troops were under the command of the Sirdar who was a servant of the Khedive.[3]

Dr. V. A. O'Rourke, the American political scientist who made a study of the juristic status of the Sudan, found it difficult to agree with the view that the territory continued to remain under the final sovereignty of Turkey. 'The complete domination of the Sudan by the Mahdists for some fifteen years', he wrote, 'appears sufficient to have extinguished whatever remnants of Turkish sovereignty remained in that region. The Sudanese made a successful revolt against Egyptian rule and became so powerful that they even attempted an invasion of Egypt, being frustrated in this only by the intervention of British troops. The Mahdists not only governed themselves without external intrusion but also were able to rout an Abyssinian army which had commenced to advance upon their territory.'[4] Further reasons given by O'Rourke to

[1] T. J. Lawrence, *Principles of International Law*, London, 1937, pp. 170-1.
[2] *Ibid.*
[3] Cromer to Lord Salisbury, 13th March, 1896, F.O. 78/4761; Lord Salisbury to British Ambassador in Turkey, 3rd June, 1896, F.O. 141/315.
[4] Vernon A. O'Rourke, *The Juristic Status of Egypt & the Sudan*, in the Johns Hopkins University Studies in Historical and Political Science, Series 53, Baltimore (1935), p. 148.

support his view were that no edict emanating from the Porte or the Khedive was enforced there, and that no taxation was imposed by anybody other than the Khalifa.

O'Rourke went as far as saying that the Sudan in that period became an independent sovereign state. Speaking of the Sudanese Government he said, 'Working together with a fairly discernible unity of purpose and obeying a common head, it can, perhaps, be maintained that not only was the Turkish sovereignty ejected but also a legal Sudanese sovereignty arose in its place. During the height of the Khalifa's supremacy, Egypt, in a measure, recognized the efficacy of his rule by a decision of the Council of Ministers on 26th April, 1888, in which the southern boundary of Egypt was fixed at a point north of the territory occupied by the Dervishes. Further than this, an Egyptian High Commissioner, Prince Hassan, was actually sent to Wadi Halfa by the Egyptian Government to make terms with the Mahdists.'[1]

When the British Government found it necessary to determine the status of the Sudan after the joint Anglo-Egyptian conquest, they were faced with the legal and political complications described above. Their solution was the 1899 Agreement. This Agreement did not resolve the obscurity of the Sudan during the rule of the Mahdi and the Khalifa. The reference in the preamble to the 'provinces of the Sudan which were in rebellion against the authority of His Highness' the Khedive indicates that the British Government admitted the survival of Egyptian—and, thus Turkish—sovereignty. On the other hand the mention of the British right of conquest implies that the Sudan was regarded as *res nullius*.

This wavering attitude, which admittedly was necessitated by the difficult circumstances of the case, led to the question, is the 1899 Agreement legally valid? Whether or not the Agreement was valid at the time of signature depends on the definition of the status of the Sudan before the conquest. Any attempt to give ruling on this matter is to indulge in a sterile academic discussion. The fact to-day is that the Agreement, which served as the constitutional charter of the Sudan for half a century, which was not questioned by the Sultan at any time, and which has never been

[1] *Ibid*, pp. 148-9.

objected to by the foreign governments who have treated with the government of the Sudan to which it gave birth, is an established legal instrument and is therefore valid. Its validity was also recognized by a Mixed Tribunal of the first instance in Cairo on 2nd April, 1910. The tribunal heard a case which involved obligations arising out of a contract between the Sudan Government and a firm of contractors. The plaintiffs sued the Egyptian Government on the grounds that the Sudan continued to be an integral part of Egypt. The Egyptian Government itself pleaded its irresponsibility and pointed to the 1899 Agreement. The court decided against the plaintiffs and proclaimed that 'so to speak a new state, distinct and separate from Egypt, has been created, which has the right of administering and legislating and judging'. The Sudan Government pleaded that the Sudan was outside the jurisdiction of the Mixed Tribunals (vide Article VIII of the 1899 Agreement) and the tribunal upheld the plea.[1]

If the Agreement was valid, then sovereignty over the Sudan became vested in Britain on the one hand and Turkey, acting through Egypt,[2] on the other. But since the Governor-General of the Sudan became the ultimate legal authority (vide Articles III and IV) and since the Sudan entered, and still enters, into agreements with Great Britain and Egypt by international procedure,[3] as well as agreements with other powers, some jurists, like Blanchard, went as far as to say that the Sudan became a sovereign state.[4] This view, however, cannot be accepted because the Governor-General is appointed and removed, not by the Sudanese at their own discretion, but by Britain and Egypt. His legal authority is also limited by the Agreement because we find that he cannot delegate his full powers to the Sudanese, in the process of training them for self-government, without authorization by the two Powers.

The nominal sovereignty of Turkey over Egypt and the Sudan continued until 1915. In this year, when Turkey entered the war

---

[1] MacMichael p. 65-6, O'Rourke, *op. cit.*, p. 156.

[2] H. Lauterpacht, *Oppenheim's International Law* London 1947, Vol. I, p. 409.

[3] Such as the agreement signed with Egypt in 1902 providing for the retention of fugitives from justice and the reciprocal acknowledgement of judicial acts, and the agreement with Britain establishing a regular exchange of money orders.

[4] Quoted by O'Rourke, *op. cit.*, p. 153.

on the side of Germany, Britain declared a protectorate over Egypt, thereby terminating Turkish sovereignty and establishing her own. No mention of the Sudan was made in the declaration of the protectorate but the termination of Turkish sovereignty over Egypt meant also its termination over the Sudan. All Turkish rights over both territories were later formally relinquished by Turkey in the Treaty of Lausanne (1923).

However, the rights of the Sultan of Egypt, as he came to be entitled, were left unchanged in spite of the protectorate. When Britain declared Egypt an independent State in 1922 the Sudan was made the subject of one of the four reservations; and when they both signed a treaty in 1936, the High Contracting Parties, while confirming the 1899 Agreement, and while reserving liberty to conclude new conventions modifying it in future, agreed that nothing in the article referring to the Sudan prejudiced the question of sovereignty over that country.[1] But where sovereignty lay was left completely unresolved. The cracks were very wide and the paper over them very thin.

[1] Treaty of Alliance between the United Kingdom and Egypt. Cmd. 5270, 1936.

CHAPTER V

THE REVIVAL OF EGYPTIAN CLAIMS

1920—1924

SOON after the establishment of the Condominium in 1899 the dispute subsided, and it was not until 1920, when Egyptian politicians in the course of their demands for independence claimed full sovereignty over the Sudan, that it was revived. Thus, the long period between 1900 and 1919, for all its importance for economic and educational development both in the Sudan and in Egypt, is to be passed over in these pages because the dispute was latent. It is only necessary to note briefly the developments which, slowly maturing in this period, affected the dispute when it was renewed.

The developments that took place in Egypt were:

1. The expansion of perennial irrigation, rendered possible by the construction of the Aswan dam and other works below it, increased Egyptian prosperity and made Egyptian population increase by leaps and bounds. It also made the question of the control of the Nile and the allocation of its waters between Egypt and the Sudan a matter of much higher importance to Egypt than the question of protecting her southern frontier against the hordes of central Africa whom she had feared in the days of Cherif Pasha.

2. Following the accession of Turkey to the side of Germany in the first world war, Great Britain declared a protectorate over Egypt and the termination of Turkish sovereignty, without making any reference to the status of the Sudan.

3. Egyptian nationalism, which was temporarily suppressed by the British occupation in 1882, and prevented from taking an extremist line by the policy of Lord Cromer during the reign of Abbas II, gained momentum during the war and emerged as an important factor in the situation in 1919. It was strengthened by the increase of prosperity and education, the ideals of freedom

and self-determination declared by President Wilson, the unduly severe action following the incident of Danshowai,[1] and the grievances of the fellaheen and the educated class during and after the war. The fellaheen resented the crude methods adopted by the British military authorities in the conscription of labour and the commandeering of animals and crops for the war effort, and the educated class bore a grudge against the British for denying them a status equal to that given to the Arabs after the war.[2]

The position in the Sudan was considerably altered. The new administration succeeded in making the Sudan financially independent of Egypt by 1913. This gave the administration practical autonomy. By the same year all the necessary investigations for the development of agriculture in the Gezira plain by means of artificial irrigation were completed, and the construction of the Sennar dam was started. This project had two main effects on the Egyptian attitude towards the Sudan. The first was that the Egyptians feared that the irrigation of the Gezira plain might interfere with their increasing demand for water necessary for maintaining Egypt's growing population. The second was that they viewed the agricultural development of the Sudan with jealousy and apprehension. It was viewed with jealousy because the British were employing millions of capital in the Sudan with high rates of interest, whereas no interest was paid on Egyptian loans.[3] It was viewed with apprehension because, in addition to the use of Nile waters, the Sudan cotton, which was to be the main crop in the Gezira, might compete with Egyptian cotton in English and world markets. There was also the feeling that the British would have a strong reason for maintaining their grip over the Sudan now that they had such important economic interests there. Lastly, as a result of the development of a new educational

---

[1] The famous Danshowai incident took place in 1906 and left a deep impression on the Egyptians. It happened when some British officers went to shoot pigeons near the village of Danshowai in Lower Egypt. The villagers interfered to prevent the shooting and an affray took place in which one officer and two villagers were killed. Five sentences of death and many sentences of imprisonment with penal servitude were passed on the villagers. (Cromer, *Abbas II*, pp. ix–x Wavell, *Allenby in Egypt*, London, 1944, p. 90; and Abdel Rahman El Rafi, *Mustafa Kemal, op. cit.*, pp. 166-80).

[2] Wavell, *Allenby in Egypt, op. cit.*, pp. 34–47. See editorial note at the end of this chapter.

[3] See Chapter IX.

system, a new generation was born in the Sudan with its own national aspirations.

In the international sphere, the British position in the Sudan, as defined in the 1899 Agreement, was neither queried nor opposed by any European powers, and their acquiescence was regarded as a recognition of that position. The only European power that had continued to resist British policy in the Sudan was France, but a settlement between her and Britain had been reached on 21st March, 1899, less than two months after the signing of the 1899 Agreement between Egypt and Britain.[1]

The fourth phase of the dispute opened immediately after the war when Egyptian leaders demanded the restoration of the Sudan to Egypt at the same time as they were agitating for the abolition of the protectorate. Neither Adly Pasha, the moderate politician, nor Zaghlul Pasha, the extremist leader of the Wafd, would agree to anything short of Egypt's full rights of sovereignty over the Sudan throughout this phase.

The question of the Sudan and the relations of Egypt and Britain with it arose four times during this period.

The first time was when the Milner Commission came to Egypt in 1920. The Commission discussed the Sudan question with the Egyptian leaders but no agreement was reached.

The second occasion was when Adly Pasha, then Prime Minister, visited London in 1921 to negotiate a settlement of the whole Egyptian question including the Sudan. Lord Curzon's proposals about the Sudan gave Egypt an undertaking to secure for her a fair share in the waters of the Nile and promised her that no more irrigation works would be constructed on the Nile south of Wadi Halfa without the concurrence of a board of three conservators representing Egypt, the Sudan and Uganda. In return Egypt was to give an undertaking to continue to contribute towards the military expenditure in the Sudan because the peaceful development of the Sudan was 'essential to the security of Egypt and the maintenance of her water supply.'[2]

---

[1] Langer, p. 570.
[2] Papers respecting negotiations with the Egyptian delegation, 1921. Cmd. 1555.

Adly Pasha refused to accept any arrangement which did 'not guarantee to Egypt her indisputable right of sovereignty over that country and the control of the waters of the Nile.'[1]

The third time was when the Egyptians were in the process of drafting their constitution after the declaration by Britain of Egyptian independence of 1922. Notwithstanding the fact that the Sudan was a reserved subject in the British declaration, the Commission appointed to draft the constitution recommended that the King should be styled the King of Egypt and the Sudan. The second article of the draft constitution read, 'Although the Sudan belongs to the Egyptian Kingdom, the constitution does not apply to it and a special administration will be provided.'[2] These recommendations were not deleted until Lord Allenby told King Fuad that unless he immediately withdrew his claim to the Sudan the British Government were determined 'to review at once and radically their recent declarations of Egyptian policy'.[3] The clause referring to the Sudan was changed and it ran as follows:—

'The present constitution is applicable to the Kingdom of Egypt. This clause does not prejudice the rights which Egypt has over the Sudan. The title which the King of Egypt will bear will be established after duly accredited delegations have fixed definitely the status of the Sudan.'[4]

The last occasion was when Zaghlul Pasha, who became the first Egyptian Prime Minister under the new constitution, visited London for talks with Mr. MacDonald in September, 1924. Mr. MacDonald had expressed sympathy with Egyptian aspirations before he came to office. This led the Egyptian public and politicians to cherish the hope that they could come to a favourable settlement with Labour leaders of the outstanding questions in the 1922 declaration of independence. They soon learned that they were no wiser in judging British policy than Abbas II and Egyptian politicians when they thought in 1892 that Mr. Gladstone's Liberal Government would immediately evacuate Egypt and

---

[1] *Ibid.*
[2] The Royal Institute of International Affairs, *Great Britain and Egypt 1914–36*, London, 1936, p. 57.
[3] Lloyd, Vol. II, p. 73.
[4] Royal Institute of International Affairs, *op. cit.*, p. 57.

give her full independence. Zaghlul Pasha was uncompromising with Mr. MacDonald in his attitude towards the Sudan and he adhered to the unstatesmanlike pronouncements which he had made in the Chamber of Deputies on 23rd June, 1924, to the effect that Egypt had complete rights of ownership over the Sudan and that the British Government were usurpers.[1] The attitude he adopted in the course of the talks which he had with Mr. Mac-Donald with a view to reaching an agreement 'rendered such agreement impossible'[2] at that stage.

While Zaghlul Pasha was having his talks with the British Prime Minister, and for some months before Zaghlul went to London, an anti-British campaign was being conducted in Egypt and in the Sudan. In Egypt the campaign took the shape of assaults against British lives, but in the Sudan it was in the form of demonstrations, riots and parades which produced a serious situation, particularly because the campaign was carried on by Egyptian and Sudanese civil servants and army officers.[3] So much anxiety was caused to the Governor-General of the Sudan and the High Commissioner in Egypt that they held a conference with Mr. MacDonald in August, 1924, to consider methods by which the disorders and the subversive Egyptian propaganda could be combated and discipline in the Egyptian army, units of which took part in the disturbances, maintained. In this conference Mr. MacDonald told the High Commissioner for Egypt and the Sudan and the Governor-General that the British Government would be prepared to tell the Egyptians that they must leave the Sudan if they insisted on causing trouble there.[4] Mr. MacDonald, following the failure of the talks he had with Zaghlul, made the British attitude towards developments in the Sudan quite clear. 'His Majesty's Government', he said 'have no desire to disturb existing arrangements, but they must point out how intolerable is a *status quo* which enables both military and civil officers and officials to conspire against civil order.'[5]

---

[1] Despatch respecting the position of His Majesty's Government in regard to Egypt and the Sudan, 1924. Cmd. 2269, also MacMichael, p. 151.

[2] *Ibid.*

[3] Lloyd, Vol. II, p. 90; also MacMichael, pp. 149–163.

[4] Lloyd, Vol. II, pp. 133-4.

[5] Cmd. 2269, 1924, *op. cit.*

The campaign, however, continued unabated until it came to a climax on 19th November, 1924. On that day an incident took place which put the clock back for Egypt in the Sudan. That was the assassination of Sir Lee Stack, the Governor-General of the Sudan and Sirdar of the Egyptian army, in Cairo. On 22nd November, after Sir Lee Stack's funeral, Lord Allenby delivered on behalf of the British Government an ultimatum to Zaghlul Pasha. The ultimatum expressed in very strong terms British anger at the crime and held Zaghlul and his Government responsible for it, because they were held either incapable or unwilling to stop the anti-British campaign in Egypt and the Sudan, about which Zaghlul had been warned by Mr. MacDonald a little over a month before the crime. The ultimatum demanded that the Egyptian Government should immediately present ample apology; inquire into the crime and punish the criminals; forbid and vigourously suppress all popular political demonstrations; pay a fine of £500,000, and order within twenty-four hours the withdrawal from the Sudan of all Egyptian officers and the purely Egyptian units of the Sudan army. It also gave warning that the Sudan Government would increase the area to be irrigated at the Gezira from 300,000 feddans (a figure which was originally agreed on with Egypt) to an unlimited figure as need might arise.[1]

Zaghlul's Government accepted the items concerning the apology, the indemnity and the punishment of the criminals but declined to accept the other demands and tendered their resignation to the King.

Allenby's ultimatum was harsh to the point of humiliation, and one of its items, that which refers to the area to be cultivated in the Gezira, was irrelevant and aroused in the Egyptian people a feeling of fear about the security of their water supply which the British Government had been careful to dispel on every occasion before the murder of Sir Lee Stack and which they have never again provoked since that event.[2] Had Allenby waited for the British Government's approval of his proposed ultimatum, the Egyptian Government would have been less humiliated. The text approved by the British Government omitted the indemnity

[1] Lloyd, Vol. II, pp. 96–7.
[2] For further comment on this item see Chapter VII.

and modified the item concerning the use of Nile waters to demanding Egyptian 'agreement to such extension of Gezira
irrigation as may be considered possible without detriment to
Egypt by technical commission containing a member appointed
by the Egyptian Government.'[1] Allenby was afraid that if he
waited for the British Government's approval, which came a few
hours later than he wanted, Zaghlul might resign and he would
have no Egyptian Government to which to deliver his terms.[2]

When Zaghlul resigned King Fuad appointed Ziwar Pasha,
who accepted and carried out the British demands. All Egyptian
troops were withdrawn from the Sudan and civil servants of
purely Egyptian blood were expelled. The only thing left for
Egypt in the Sudan was the Egyptian flag. It thus resembled the
flag of Turkey, which flew unmolested on a rock in Suda Bay in
Crete from 1898 to 1912 while a High Commissioner appointed
by four European powers ruled the island, and the people had
freedom to cultivate as close relations with Greece as they pleased.[3]
Even the Egyptian flag would have been lowered but for the
stand which Allenby made.[4]

The dispute during this phase was confined to Egypt and Great
Britain, as Turkey ceased to be a party in it after the 1923 Treaty
of Lausanne, in which she relinquished all rights of sovereignty
over Egypt and the Sudan.

[1] Lloyd, Vol. II, p. 98.
[2] Wavell, op. cit., p. 112.
[3] T. J. Lawrence, op. cit., pp. 72-3.
[4] Wavell, op. cit., p. 117.
  Editorial Note. The Author's reference to the emergence of Egyptian nationalism
hardly brings out how much the improvement of the fellaheen to which he refers was
due to the great remedial influence of Lord Cromer over the administration and
finance of the country.

CHAPTER VI

THE NILE WATERS AND
THE RESTORATION OF PRE-1924 STATUS

(1925—1936)

AS soon as the wave of British anger over the assassination of Sir Lee Stack subsided, Ziwar Pasha proceeded to request Lord Allenby (26th January, 1925) to reconsider the question of irrigation in the Gezira which 'had raised the most serious apprehensions'[1] in Egypt. Allenby answered on the same day assuring him of the good intentions of the British Government and informing him that they were 'disposed to direct the Sudan Government not to give effect to the previous instructions in regard to the unlimited development of the Sudan Gezira.'[2] He further suggested the setting up of an expert committee for the purpose of examining and proposing the basis on which irrigation could be carried on in the Sudan without detriment to Egypt's interests and rights.

The committee made its investigations and submitted its report which formed the basis of an agreement which, thanks to the statesmanship of Mohammed Mahmud Pasha, was signed in 1929 without waiting for the settlement of the whole Sudan question. This agreement solved the technical side of the Nile waters question for Egypt but the political side continued to be an obstacle in the way of a final settlement of the whole question.[3]

Negotiation for the settlement of the 'reserved subjects' in the 1922 declaration of Egyptian independence, which included the Sudan, were not resumed until late in 1927. Attempts to resume such negotiations were not made earlier because, in addition to the situation created by the assassination of Sir Lee Stack, Egypt was suffering from the political and constitutional crises which

[1] Exchange of notes—in regard to the use of the waters of the River Nile for irrigation purposes, 1929. Cmd. 3348, p. 33.
[2] *Ibid.*
[3] See Chapter VII.

usually befall a nation just beginning to experience rule by a constitutional monarchy. There was continuous friction between the Prime Minister, Zaghlul, and King Fuad over the limits of the King's powers, and the cleavage between the two men was widened by the personal dislike which each felt for the other. So when Zaghlul resigned after the Lee Stack incident, the King took the opportunity and ruled the country for nearly two years through Ziwar Pasha, who was loyal to him, without a parliament. It must be noted also that Allenby's disapproval of Zaghlul gave the King strong reasons to justify his removal. In fact Zaghlul never resumed his office as prime minister even after the restoration of parliamentary life and the success of his party at the polls. Coalition governments under minority leaders had to be formed because no enduring reconciliation between the King and Zaghlul was possible.[1] This lack of stability contributed to the failure of attempts to reach a settlement with Britain by the minority leaders, Sarwat and Mahmud, in 1927 and 1929. The same kind of crisis also contributed to the failure of the later attempt in 1946, when the relations obtaining between King Farouk and Nahas Pasha were even more strained than those between his father and the first leader of the Wafd.

Three attempts to reach a settlement were made between 1927 and 1930 but they were all abortive. The first was made by Sarwat Pasha, who succeeded Adly as head of the second coalition government, and Mr. Chamberlain. They agreed on a settlement of the first three reserved subjects and deferred the question of the Sudan to a later date.[2] But when Sarwat returned to Egypt he failed to secure the support of the leaders of the majority, and the proposals were shelved.

The second attempt was made by Mohammed Mahmud Pasha and Mr. Henderson in 1929. They again deferred the final settlement of the Sudan question to a later date but agreed that the status of the Sudan should be that resulting from the 1899 agreement. Provisions were also made for the settlement by the Sudan Government of the sum of about £E.4,000,000 advanced by Egypt

[1] Abdel Rahman El Rafi, *The Years Following the Egyptian Revolution* (Arabic), Cairo, 1947, Vol. I, pp. 209–276; Wavell, *op. cit.*, pp. 84, 86, 95, 97, 117 & 119.
[2] Papers regarding negotiations for a Treaty of Alliance with Egypt, 1928. Cmd. 3050.

between 1901 and 1909 for railway building and the construction
of Port Sudan, for the application of international conventions to
the Sudan, and for the return to the Sudan of an Egyptian battal-
ion.[1] Mahmud returned to Egypt and held a general election
during which he made the treaty proposals the main issue. But
Mahmud Pasha, who had suspended the constitution and ruled
Egypt as a dictator, was unpopular and suffered a heavy defeat.
Nothing therefore came out of his proposals.

The third attempt was made in 1930 by Nahas Pasha and Mr.
Henderson. As Nahas Pasha was the first prime minister to
command support in the Egyptian parliament since the conversations of Mr. MacDonald with Zaghlul Pasha, there seemed to be
some hope of his coming to an agreement and getting support for
it in parliament. But he and Mr. Henderson failed to reach agreement. The point on which the negotiations seem to have broken
down was the introduction of a totally new issue in the dispute.
The increase in Egyptian population became alarming by 1930,[2]
and the Egyptian delegation insisted on unrestricted emigration
to the Sudan as a possible solution of this problem. This the British
delegation refused to accept. But a close study of the documents
on these talks[3] shows that the negotiations broke down because
the Egyptian delegation failed to secure recognition of Egypt's
right of sovereignty over the Sudan, and to get the British delegation to agree to that joint Anglo-Egyptian administration of the
country which the Agreement of 1899 had foreshadowed and
which had, in fact, even before 1924, never been carried out.

It was not until the world political situation became grave that
both parties showed readiness to give and take.[4] The overrunning
of Ethiopia by Italy and the menace of the Rome-Berlin Axis to
the safety of the Mediterranean and the Suez Canal made it
imperative on the British Government to be more lenient with
Egypt, and created a situation which compelled Egyptian statesmen to be less intransigent. The compromise which provided a

---

[1] Exchange of notes relating to Proposals for an Anglo-Egyptain settlement, 1929.
Cmd. 3376.

[2] See below pp. 78, and 89ff.

[3] Papers regarding the recent negotiations for an Anglo-Egyptian settlement,
1930. Cmd. 3575.

[4] The Royal Institute of International Affairs, op. cit., p. 46.

temporary solution to all the outstanding problems formed the 1936 Treaty of Alliance and Friendship.[1]

Only Article 11 of the 1936 Treaty deals with the Sudan, but, as the dispute between Britain and Egypt over Egypt's independence and other Anglo-Egyptian relations affects the Sudan question,[2] it is important to give a short review of this treaty.

The treaty safeguarded for Great Britain her strategic and economic interests in the Mediterranean by providing that one party should give aid to the other if either party becomes engaged in war (Article 7). The aid which Egypt was required to give consisted of facilities on Egyptian territory for British land, sea and air forces. Egypt stood by her treaty obligations in the last war and the treaty proved to be a satisfactory settlement for the British Government. In addition to the war-time facilities the treaty provided for the stationing of British military and air forces in time of peace in the Canal Zone 'with a view to ensuring, in co-operation with the Egyptian forces, the defence of the Canal' until such time as the High Contracting Parties should agree that the Egyptian Army had become capable of defending the Canal without outside help (Article 8).

For Egypt the treaty rectified the defects of the 1922 declaration of Egyptian independence by liquidating three of the four subjects that were reserved to the discretion of the British Government. 'The Security of Communications of the British Empire in Egypt' became a joint responsibility of the British and Egyptian forces; 'the defence of Egypt against all foreign aggression or interference direct or indirect' became Egypt's sole responsibility and Egypt entered into a treaty of alliance with Britain; 'the protection of foreign interests in Egypt and the protection of minorities' was no longer left to the discretion of the British Government. Britain, by the provisions of the Treaty, undertook to assist Egypt in getting rid of the system of the capitulations. A conference was held of all the powers in Montreux in 1937 during which agreement was reached on the abolition of the system.

The Sudan which formed the fourth reserved subject was dealt with in Article 11 which laid down that the administration of the

---

[1] Cmd. 5270, *op. cit.*
[2] See below pp. 116–117.

Sudan shall continue to be that resulting from the 1899 Agreement without prejudice to the question of Egyptian sovereignty. It made no specific reference to Egyptian participation in the administration of the Sudan, but provided for the selection of suitable British or Egyptian nationals to posts for which no qualified Sudanese could be found. It also provided for the return to the Sudan of two Egyptian battalions, raised all restriction on Egyptian immigration except for reasons of public health and public order, and agreed upon the desirability and acceptability of inviting the Inspector-General of Egyptian irrigation service in the Sudan to attend meetings of the Governor-General's Council when matters relating to his departmental interests came before the council.

A notable addition to the provisions of the 1899 Agreement was also introduced in the Sudan article. The High Contracting parties agreed 'that the primary aim of their administration in the Sudan must be the welfare of the Sudanese'. This is the first time that Britain and Egypt officially defined the aim of their administration. It is a vague definition which, as will be shown, led to serious disagreement in the later stage of the dispute.

The 1936 treaty was well received in Egypt and came to be known as 'the treaty of honour and independence'. Thus the fifth phase of the dispute appeared to end happily for both parties.

PART TWO

THE ELEMENTS
OF THE DISPUTE

CHAPTER VII

THE CONTROL AND ALLOCATION OF NILE WATERS

THE 1936 treaty affords an excellent point at which to pause in our account of the dispute, and before proceeding to examine its latest phase, to discuss the main issues at stake and assess their influence upon those on whom falls the task of making a settlement.

The first element of the dispute which we must consider is the question of the Nile, that great river which intrigued Herodotus, fascinated the Arab conqueror 'Amr Ibn El 'Ass, caught the imagination of Winston Churchill, and gave present day Egyptains and some Sudanese their attractive political slogan 'the Unity of the Nile Valley.' Yet the Nile, which appears to the young patriot to unite the two countries in the same way as a string threads together the beads of a necklace, has gradually become a source of contention between Egypt and the Sudan, and the problems of controlling it and allocating its waters for purposes of irrigation have become the main question that preoccupies the mind of the Egyptian statesman and negotiator.

We have seen how Egypt's interests in the Sudan were strategic and commercial in the earlier stages of the dispute. But it became apparent, not long after the establishment of the new administrative regime in the Sudan, that its predominantly British Government was embarking upon the agricultural development of an area of some considerable size by means of artificial irrigation from the Nile. As this project might not only interfere seriously with Egypt's ever-increasing water requirements, but might put Egypt's own irrigation under control from the Sudan, the question of the control of the Nile and the allocation of its waters became a main subject of the dispute. Indeed, it became the primary reason why the Egyptians have agitated ever since the beginning of the nationalist movement for absolute sovereignty over the Sudan.

73

Professor Toynbee considers the importance of the Nile to Egypt analogous to that of the Suez Canal to the British Empire.[1] In fact the control of the Nile is far more important to the existence of Egypt than the Suez Canal is to the British Empire. The experience of the two world wars has shown that the closure of the Suez Canal, although it added a heavy financial burden and wasted much valuable time, did not mean the severing of communications between the United Kingdom and those parts of the Commonwealth that lay in the East. But the control of the Nile in Uganda, Ethiopia and the Sudan, and the free use of its waters for irrigation and other purposes such as hydro-electric schemes, regardless of Egypt's interests or with a view to subjecting her, might cost the 'Gift of the Nile' her very existence.

Egypt's interests in the Nile at present are based upon both economic and political grounds.

Economically Egypt depends to-day, as she always did, almost entirely on agriculture. And, being a country with no rainfall over most of her surface, and with negligible amounts in the rest, her agriculture depends entirely on the Nile.

No complicated problems arose in the past when Egyptian agriculture depended on the floods and on primitive methods of irrigation and when the peoples inhabiting the upper basin of the river relied much more on the rains for their agriculture than on the river. Egypt was always assured of her supply of water except, of course, when the floods were exceptionally low. But since modern engineering knowledge rendered possible the harnessing of the Nile for purposes of expanding perennial irrigation in Egypt, and since the Sudan began to follow Egypt's example in agricultural development, a complicated problem of control and allocation of waters ensued. A slight further complication arose in 1949 when Uganda decided to build a dam at Owen Falls, for the production of hydro-electric power. Egypt voted £E.4,500,000 towards the cost of this dam in order to safeguard her interests by establishing rights in this dam. Uganda contributed £7½ million as a preliminary payment.[2]

---

[1] Toynbee, pp. 234-5.
[2] Announcement by the British Foreign Secretary in the House of Commons on 19th May, 1949. Debates 5th Series., Vol. 465, col. 620.

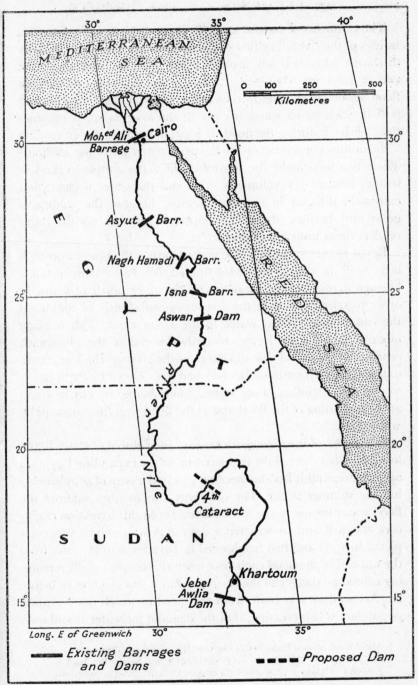

THE CONTROL OF THE NILE NORTH OF KHARTOUM

The problems of control and allocation arose out of two pecul-
iarities of the river. The first of these is that the volume of its daily
discharge when it is low (from the beginning of February to the
end of July) may be one-twentieth of the discharge during the
flood season (from August to October or November).[1] The second
is that, whereas its water is clear in the low season, it becomes
thick with silt during the flood. It is estimated that the silt reaches
a maximum concentration in Egypt of 2,500 parts per million.[2]
These two facts make the control of the water simple in the low
season, because the volume is small and the water is clear, and
extremely difficult in the flood season, because the volume is
great and because the accumulation of silt behind the dams
renders them unfit for storing water.

Egypt began to control Nile waters during the low season on a
large scale in 1843, when Mohammed Ali Pasha constructed a
barrage across the two branches of the river north of Cairo in
order to raise its level in the low season sufficiently to command
the canals that carried water to the Delta areas. This barrage
made it possible for Egypt, towards the end of the nineteenth
century, to use up all the discharge of the river in the low season
so that the two mouths of the river had to be closed by earth banks
to prevent the influx of sea water. These banks are cut by hand
at the beginning of the flood and as the flood rises they are rapidly
washed out.[3]

By the end of the nineteenth century the volume of water in the
low season fell short of the requirements of the expanding Egyptian
agriculture, and it became necessary to find a way of supplement-
ing the summer water. The only way was to store some of the
flood water for use in the low seasons. To do this irrigation engineers designed and constructed a dam at Aswan, which was completed in 1902 and first heightened in 1912 for storing water from
the tail end of the flood each year when the amount of silt remaining caused no danger to the reservoir. But it was clear, even before
the Aswan dam was built, from the speed at which the Egyptian
population was increasing, that the demand for water would soon

[1] Abdel Kawi Ahmed Pasha in *The Engineers Magazine*, Cairo, May, 1948.
[2] H. E. Hurst in *Civil Engineering and Public Works Review*, September, 1948.
[3] J. A. de C. Hamilton, *op. cit.* Note the chapter by R. M. MacGregor, p. 284.

overtake the supply, even after the heightening of the dam. So the Ministry of Works undertook extensive surveys with a view to drawing plans for meeting the eventual demands.[1]

Shortly after the heightening of the Aswan dam, and before Egypt took further measures for increasing her water supply, the Sudan Government started in 1913 to build a dam across the Blue Nile in the Sudan for irrigating a part of the two million feddans of the Sudan Gezira, which are capable of development.

The Sudan Government's action brought before the eyes of the Egyptians the possibility of the greatest danger that ever threatened their prosperity and their future. The policy of developing the Sudan Gezira appeared to Egyptian statesmen to threaten, in the first place, Egypt's present and future requirements of Nile water, especially if the Sudan were to use all or some of the discharge of the Blue Nile in the low season. They argued that the Sudan had no right to use any water over which Egypt had established a right which they dated from the time she began to use all the summer water of the Nile. The argument is based on the occidental practice of 'first in time first in right'.[2] They also argued that the Sudan, which relied on the rains for growing its cotton and other crops, should not embark upon an artificial irrigation scheme before all the possibilities of rain cultivation had been fully exploited.[3]

In the second place, the Gezira scheme, which was intended for the purpose of growing long staple cotton, caused some anxiety that at some future date cotton production in the Sudan might turn out to be detrimental to Egyptian interests in world cotton markets.[4]

Egypt's continuous anxiety about the necessary water for her agricultural expansion to support a rapidly increasing population and to keep a favourable balance of trade, and her anxiety about possible competition in cotton markets, will be well understood in the light of the following figures:—

[1] Reports by Sir William Garstin, most important of which is his 3rd Report, 1904.
[2] Abdel Kawi Ahmed Pasha *op. cit.*, p. 13.
[3] Toynbee, p. 260.
[4] Abbas Hilmi *A Few Words on the Anglo-Egyptian Settlement*, London, 1930, p. 28.

Land and Population in Egypt[1]

Year	Cultivated area in mn. feddans	Crop area in mn. feddans	Population in millions	Cultivated area per head of population in feddans	Crop area per head of population in feddans
1800	3·0	3·0	2·5	1·2	1·2
1877	4·75	4·75	6·44	0·74	0·74
1897	5·09	6·85	9·63	0·53	0·71
1907	5·4	7·6	11·3	0·48	0·67
1917	5·3	7·8	12·8	0·41	0·61
1927	5·5	8·6	14·2	0·39	0·61
1937	5·3	8·5	15·9	0·33	0·53
1940	5·2	8·5	16·8	0·31	0·50

These figures show that while the cultivated area remained the same, the crop area showed a remarkable increase. This is due to the practice of growing two crops a year, rendered possible by storage of flood water for use in the summer. The increase in population, however, caused a steady decrease in the crop area per head of the population.

The figures of Egyptian trade also show how vital agriculture is to Egypt. Cotton, cotton-seed and cotton-seed oil have always been the main items of Egyptian export trade. The total value of cotton and cotton-seed exports was 83 per cent of the total value of Egyptian exports in 1888.[2] The percentage went up to 94 in the 1913-14 season, and in 1937 it was 80 per cent.[3]

The following table shows how Egyptian imports fluctuate with the fluctuation in cotton prices[4]:—

[1] For 1800–1897 cultivated area figures see Issawi p. 14 and *The National Bank of Egypt 1898–1948*, Cairo, 1949, p. 10; for crop area over same period see *The National Bank of Egypt 1898–1948*, p. 10 and Issawi p. 60; for population figures Issawi p. 44. For all figures for 1907–1940 see Hurst, Black and Simaika, p. 13.

[2] *The National Bank of Egypt 1898–1948*, Cairo, 1949 (Arabic), p. 24.

[3] Issawi, pp. 112–114.

[4] *The National Bank of Egypt 1898–1948*, Cairo, 1949, pp. 140–143.

Year	Price of Kantar in $	Total imports in Egyptian Pounds
1900/01	13·80	15,245,000
1901/02	10·42	14,815,000
1918/19	37·20	47,407,000
1919/20	87·81	101,150,000
1930/31	12·04	31,275,000
1931/32	10·08	27,262,000
1946/47	42·28	103,902,000

Egypt, therefore, strongly opposed the Sudan Gezira scheme,[1] agitated for the control of the whole river from Cairo,[2] and insisted on full sovereignty over the Sudan.[3] The Sudan Government, however, went ahead with the construction of the Sennar dam on the Blue Nile and the work, which was interrupted by the first World War, was completed in 1925. But Lord Allenby, then High Commissioner for Egypt and the Sudan, in order to dispel Egyptian fears about indefinite use of the Blue Nile Waters, gave Egypt an undertaking in February, 1920, that the area to be irrigated in the Gezira would not exceed 300,000 feddans.[4]

Meanwhile the British and Egyptian engineers were busy working out a scheme of Nile projects for storing water to meet the increasing requirements of Egypt and the Sudan as well as a basis for the allocation of waters to both countries. The work was started by Sir William Garstin early in the twentieth century and a complete scheme was prepared by Sir Murdoch MacDonald in 1920.[5] The full plan included, in addition to the Aswan and Sennar dam, Jebel Awlia dam, on the White Nile some thirty miles south of Khartoum, a dam at the Equatorial Lakes, a third on Lake Tana, and a cut through the *Sudd* area to prevent the heavy loss of water which occurs in the swamps of that region. An

[1] Toynbee, pp. 254–5.
[2] *Ibid.*, p. 262–3, and Abdel Kawi Ahmed Pasha *op. cit.*
[3] See above pp. 59–60.
[4] Toynbee, p. 262.
[5] Murdoch MacDonald, *Nile Control*, Cairo, 1920.

additional proposal was made later to construct a dam on the main Nile near Merowe in the Northern Sudan. Although this dam would help in storing water for irrigation purposes, the main reason behind it was the protection of Egypt against exceptionally high floods.

The volumes of water that projects planned by Sir Murdoch MacDonald were intended to hold were:—

	Capacity in Milliard Cubic Metres (1 milliard = 1,000 million)
Aswan, Sennar and Jebel Awlia (constructed)	8
Equatorial Lakes (under construction)	5
Lake Tana (proposed)	2
TOTAL	15

When these volumes are added to the average natural river supply in the low season (February—July), which is $15\frac{1}{2}$ milliards, and when the capacity of the additional main Nile dam, which is 3 milliards, is added, the total volume which would be available for irrigation in Egypt and the Sudan would be $33\frac{1}{2}$ milliards.[1] This is 4 milliards more than the $29\frac{1}{2}$ milliards considered to be necessary for irrigating the maximum cultivable area of 7.96 million feddans[2] in Egypt and an area of 2 million feddans in the Sudan.

Sir Murdoch MacDonald's plans were examined by the Nile Projects Commission which was appointed by the Egyptian and British Governments. The Commission was composed of a nominee of the Government of India (Chairman), a nominee of the University of Cambridge, and a nominee of the Government of the United States. The Commission was requested to 'give to the Egyptian Government its opinion on the projects . . . with a view to the further regulation of the Nile supply for the benefit of Egypt and the Sudan,' and in particular 'to report upon the propriety of the manner in which, as a result of these projects, the increased supply of available water provided by them will be allocated at each stage of development between Egypt and the Sudan'.[3]

[1] H. E. Hurst *op. cit.*
[2] Hurst, Black and Simaika, pp. 10–11.
[3] *Report of the Nile Projects Commission*, 1920, p. 5.

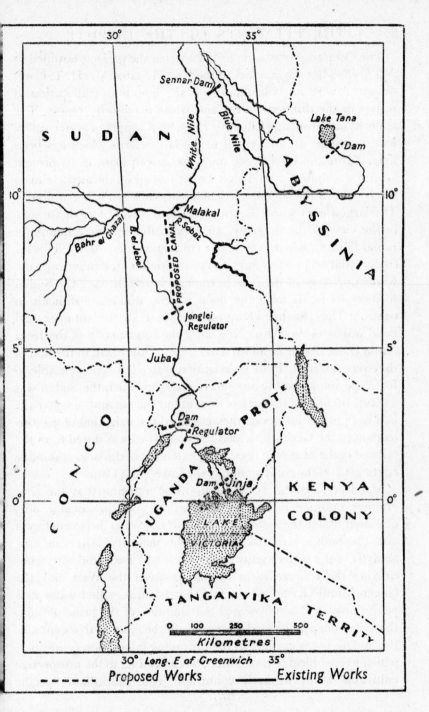

THE CONTROL OF THE NILE SOUTH OF KHARTOUM

The Commission unanimously endorsed the projects outlined in *Nile Control*, but the nominee of the United States, Mr. H. T. Cory, disagreed with his colleagues over the question of allocation of waters in the different stages and wrote a minority report. The majority acknowledged Egypt's right 'to a supply of water sufficient to irrigate an area equal to the largest area which has been irrigated in any single year since the Aswan Dam in its present form was completed, and that Egypt has an established claim to receive this water at the particular seasons when it is required'.[1] The largest area which Egypt established a right to irrigate was, in the view of the majority, an area of five million feddans (in round figures), which was under cultivation in 1916–17. This recommendation in effect gave Egypt the right to use practically the whole discharge of the Nile in the low season, leaving the Sudan to meet its needs from the flood waters, which are difficult to control. They further recommended that all the summer and flood waters of the White Nile, after the construction of the Jebel Awlia Dam, should be allotted to Egypt. With regard to the Sudan they recognized its right to irrigation water but were not able to fix in specific terms the amount of water to which the Sudan was entitled because of the lack of data about the amount of water she had been using. However, they endorsed the irrigation of 300,000 feddans in the Gezira provided the water used was stored from the tail end of the Blue Nile flood. Any extension of this area was made contingent on the construction of the Lake Tana Dam.

Mr. Cory, on the other hand, while agreeing that the programme outlined in *Nile Control* was the only practicable one, dissented about the system of allocation of water between Egypt and the Sudan recommended by the majority. After an able analysis of the water rights in the West and East, and after considering the differences in rainfall between the West and the barren Middle East, and the fact that Islam regarded water as a public property, he advocated the adoption of the principle that the as yet unappropriated waters should be allotted to Egypt and the Sudan, not according to the prevailing population conditions, which were subject to fluctuation, but according to the prospective cultivable lands in both countries. The immediate specific

[1] *Ibid.*, p. 57.

recommendation which he made was that 'the excess water over and above such vested rights (i.e. the rights already established) should be divided equally between Egypt and the Sudan'. The 'right of the Sudan', he added, 'to use Jebel Awlia water not required by Egypt when able to pay for it' must be admitted. This he recommended to avoid the Sudan losing 'a good opportunity of further development in the near future without prejudice to Egypt'.[1]

His colleagues, while they felt that his findings might be theoretically correct, considered that it was impossible 'on financial and other points to apply them in the present circumstances'.[2]

The political situation in Egypt at the time of the submission of the report (August, 1920) was not favourable to an agreement on the matter and the Egyptian Government decided in May, 1921 to suspend all irrigation works pending an agreement on the political status of the Sudan.[3] The political situation later deteriorated,[4] and a settlement of the question was not attempted until 1925 when another Committee consisting of a representative of the Egyptian Government, a representative of the British Government, and an independent Chairman was appointed 'for the purpose of examining and proposing the basis on which irrigation can be carried out with full consideration of the interests of Egypt and without detriment to her natural and historic rights'.[5] They agreed on a basis of allocation on the lines of the majority recommendation of the Nile Projects Commission and their recommendations formed the Nile Waters Agreement signed on 7th May, 1929. An important amendment, which they made to the recommendations of the Nile Projects Commission, was that the Sudan should have a specified quota of Blue Nile flood water rather than be allowed to irrigate a fixed area of 300,000 feddans. The Sudan was allotted a net volume of 929 million cubic metres, or just under one milliard cubic metres.[6] This is under 1/22 of Egypt's share. This amendment was in the interests of economy and easy control of water.

The Nile Waters Agreement guaranteed for Egypt her irrigation

[1] *Ibid.*, pp. 59–77.
[2] *Ibid.*, p. 57.
[3] Toynbee, p. 262.
[4] See above Chapter v.
[5] Cmd. 3348, 1920, *op. cit.*, p. 6.
[6] Sudan Assembly, Second Session, Vol. IV, 13th March, 1950, p. 21.

interests, and, since the completion of the Jebel Awlia dam in 1937, all Egyptian demands for water have been met. When all the irrigation works on the Nile are completed Egypt will be assured of all the waters for the land she can possibly cultivate.

With the Sudan the case is different. With the increase of the population from under an estimated 3 millions in 1899 to just under 8 millions in 1947,[1] and with the introduction of capital, agricultural expansion proceeded at such a speed that the demand for water, as predicted by Mr. Cory, overtook the supply provided by the 1929 agreement. 'The Sudan's need for more water for irrigation', said the Governor-General in his speech at the opening of the second session of the Legislative Assembly, on 6th March, 1950 'is becoming increasingly urgent and steps are being taken to secure further supplies.'[2] The work on the expansion of the Gezira from 900,000 to 1 million feddans is proceeding quickly.[3] In addition the total area of land irrigated perennially by pumps was 105,500 feddans in 1944[4] and since then pump irrigation has expanded to such an extent that all water allotted for pump schemes has been appropriated except for a small volume of 5.5 million cubic metres which is kept as a reserve.[5] The future position may be much worse even after the irrigation works programme is completed, because the population of the country is increasing. Moreover the cultivable areas in the Gezira and in the other regions which lie away from it along the White Nile and in the Upper Nile and Northern Provinces and along the east bank of the Blue Nile is, to say the least, more than three times the original area of 2 million feddans in the Gezira taken into consideration when the first estimates were made.

The problem of the allocation of Nile waters seems, therefore, to be one that will cause much friction between Egypt and the Sudan in the not very distant future. It should be noted that it is mainly because of the possibilities of agricultural expansion in the Sudan that Egypt insisted on the control of the Nile from Cairo, and, indeed, on full sovereignty over the Sudan.

---

[1] *Foreign Trade Report*, p. 173.
[2] Sudan Assembly, Second Session, Vol. I, p. 2.
[3] *Ibid.*
[4] J. D. Tothill, *op. cit.*, p. 615.
[5] Sudan Assembly, Second Session, Vol. IV, 13th March, 1950, p. 21.

There is yet another water problem which awaits solution between Egypt and the Sudan. That is the problem of protecting Egypt from the dangers of exceptionally high floods which cause more anxiety to Egypt than exceptionally low floods. The record flood of 1946 may be taken as an example of what Egypt may be exposed to in such years. Technical engineering evidence shows that, had all the water that passed Khartoum between 12th August and 11th September of that year arrived in Egypt, the whole of lower Egypt would have been turned into a lake.[1] What happened was that out of the 26·5 milliard cubic metres which passed Khartoum in this period, only 23·8 reached Hassanab, south of Atbara in the Sudan. The difference of 2·7 milliards was spilled in the low areas lying along the Nile between Tumaniat, north of Khartoum, and Hassanab,[2] causing damage to 4,400 houses and very extensive damage to the crops.[3] The water which flooded the low lands along the river in this reach was equal to the volume of water stored in the Aswan dam in 1947.

The alternatives for protecting Egypt against such a flood which were considered by Egyptian engineers before they discovered this natural method of protection were too expensive for Egypt to attempt. One of them was the heightening of the Jebel Awlia dam to hold abnormal volumes of Blue Nile flood which were to be drained into the White Nile behind the dam by means of a canal. The latest plan is to construct a dam on the main Nile near Merowe in the Northern Sudan. Until this dam is constructed Egypt is most anxious that no flood protection banks should be built in the Tumaniat-Hassanab reach. Egypt would like to see this reach exposed to floods without even accepting liability when the damage is done. All she did was to give of her own free will a sum of £E.28,000 for the relief of those affected by the flood, while the losses in the Northern Province alone, in which the Tumaniat-Hassanab reach lies, were calculated at £E.2,000,000.[4]

This is yet another cause for future friction and a reason for Egypt's agitation for controlling the Sudan. The construction of

---

[1] Abdel Kawi Ahmed Pasha, *op. cit.*, Hurst, Black and Simaika, p. 106.

[2] *Ibid.* Also Hurst, Black and Simaika, p. 106.

[3] *Sudan Monthly Record*, August–September, 1946, Section 6798.

[4] Annual Report, 1946, p. 11.

the Nile dam at Merowe will solve Egypt's problem but will leave the question of flood protection in the Sudan unsolved.

Turning to the political aspect of this question of Nile Control, Egypt fears to-day, more than she ever did before, the control of the Nile in the upper basin, in times of crises, by a strong hand. Such control will keep Egypt firmly under the thumb of the controlling power. The fear of this control is very old, but in olden days it was more legendary than real. One of the stories about the tributes which Egyptian kings paid to kings of Ethiopia, enumerated by Langer, is:—

> 'The Soldan, King of the Egyptian Land,
> Pays tribute to this sovereign, as his head,
> They say, since having Nile at his command
> He may divert the stream to other bed,
> Hence, with its district upon either hand,
> Forthwith might Cairo lack its daily bread.'[1]

The possibilities of Nile control became real towards the end of the nineteenth century, when European powers took interest in Egypt after the digging of the Suez Canal. The first European to stress the political aspect of Nile control was Sir Samuel Baker. He was anxious that Great Britain should occupy the Sudan, because, should she be forced to evacuate Egypt, she could control her from the Sudan by controlling the Nile.[2] A second strong expression of opinion on the subject came from a French engineer in the service of the Khedive, by the name of Victor Prompt. He gave an address in 1893 to the Egyptian Institute on certain problems of the hydrology of the Nile in which he suggested that 'a power in command of the Upper Nile could build barrages which, if opened, could drown the whole of Egypt.'[3] He pointed out that the dams he had in mind could be erected at the outlets of Lakes Victoria and Albert, or at the confluence of the Sobat and the White Nile, and that they could be constructed for about half a million francs apiece.[4] This lecture set President Carnot, who was an old school friend of M. Prompt, thinking seriously of occupying

[1] Langer, pp. 103–105. The verse is from *The Orlando Furioso*, (Ariosto, 16th century) translated by William S. Rose (New edition, London, 1858) Canto XXXIII, stanza cvi.

[2] T. Douglas Murray and A. Silva White, *op. cit.*, p. 373.

[3] Langer, p. 575.

[4] *Ibid.*, p. 127.

the Upper Nile regions to frighten the British out of Egypt by threatening Egypt's water supply.[1]

The British Governments were alive to these possibilities and were careful to include in the agreements signed with Powers where sources of the Nile tributaries lay, an article which bound those powers not to construct, or allow to be constructed, any work which might sensibly modify the flow of the streams into the Nile except with the agreement of His Majesty's Government.[2]

But although Great Britain struggled with success to keep all European Powers away from the Upper Nile Basin, and made sure that no works were to be constructed on the sources of the river without her consent, she did so in order to protect her position in Egypt and not for the purpose of finding a method of bringing pressure to bear upon Egypt. There was nothing, till 23rd November, 1924, to make Egypt have any suspicions about the British using their position and influence in the upper regions of the Nile to bring political pressure on her. On that date, as we have seen, the Allenby ultimatum, with the reference it included to the use of Nile waters in the Sudan,[3] brought about a strong feeling of mistrust which still prevails. The reference to the use of Nile waters in the Sudan strengthened Egyptian feeling that so long as the British stayed in the Sudan, Egypt would be under the mercy of Britain. Egyptians, therefore, consider that unless the control of the whole river is vested in Egypt, and unless the British evacuate the Sudan, Egyptian independence, even if all British troops were evacuated from Egypt, will always be dependent upon British goodwill.

When Allenby was asked why he included the reference to the Nile waters, his argument was that it 'was included to impress on Egypt the power we could wield if necessary by our control of the Sudan'.[4] He has indeed succeeded in doing this, but the result is continuous mistrust. The blame falls on Allenby's shoulders more than it does on the British Government's, because, had he waited

[1] *Ibid.*, p. 128.
[2] Sir E. Hertzlet, *op. cit.* Great Britain and Italy (15th April, 1891) Vol. III, p. 950. Great Britain and Abyssinia (15th May, 1902) Vol. II, p. 432. Great Britain and Belgian Congo (9th May, 1906) Vol. II, p. 585.
[3] See above p. 63.
[4] Wavell, *op. cit.*, p. 114.

for their approval of his proposed ultimatum, which was not given to this clause, a lot of ill-feeling would have been avoided.[1] The Egyptians did not forget this and they will never forget it. Their papers bring up the question whenever irrigation and other works on the Nile are brought to execution. The main reason for the opposition to the Jebel Awlia dam was political and the opposition to the Owen Falls dam is also made on political grounds.[2]

This question of Nile waters must, therefore, be taken into consideration when a discussion of the dispute in its most recent stage is made.

[1] See above pp. 63–64.
[2] See *Sawt El Umma* (Wafd organ) 30th November, 1948, *El Balagh* (Wafd organ) 18th January, 1949, *Al Ahram* (independent) 19th January, 1949 and 1st March, 1949, and *El Kotla* (independent Wafd) 21st May, 1949.

CHAPTER VIII

EGYPT'S OTHER INTERESTS IN THE SUDAN

EGYPT'S vital interests in the waters of the Nile were discussed in the previous Chapter, and it remains to show here what other interests in the Sudan she has which of late years have had a strong bearing on the dispute.

The introduction and expansion of the system of perennial irrigation, with the establishment of a stabel system of administration, resulted in such a rapid increase in Egyptian population between 1897 and the present day that Egypt is faced with the most serious problem of over-population that can confront a rural country. And unless this problem is properly attended to, the standard of living of the Egyptian peasant will be brought down to starvation level. It is for this reason that Egypt looks to the Sudan as a means of salvation.

Reference was made to this problem in the previous Chapter in connection with the need for more water for irrigation, but it is a problem which deserves a more detailed treatment. The total population of Egypt, which was just over $9\frac{1}{2}$ millions in 1897, rose to just under 16 millions in 1937—an increase of 6·5 millions, or 68 per cent, in 40 years. The figure rose to 17 millions in 1948, and, by Issawi's estimate, a rate of growth of 1 per cent per annum is to be expected.[1] This will bring the figure to 20 million within fifteen or twenty years from 1947. According to other estimates the figure may reach 24 million by 1962,[2] or $20\frac{1}{2}$ million by 1960.[3] Of the total population of 16 millions in 1937, 81·5 per cent lived in rural areas causing the density of population per square mile of cultivated land, which is the inhabitable part of Egypt, to be 1,450.[4] This figure is more than twice as high as that of industrial

[1] Issawi, p. 47.
[2] A Bonne, *The Economic Development of the Middle East*, London, 1945, p. 25.
[3] Hurst, Black and Simaika, p. 12.
[4] Doreen Warriner, *Land and Poverty in the Middle East*, London, 1948, p. 26.

countries in Europe. For example England and Wales have a density of 672 to the square mile.[1] It is also ten times as high as the average density of population in Europe and five times as high as that of Eastern Europe.[2] The land available for agricultural production was 8.5 million feddans in 1937, i.e. 0·53 feddans per head. There is, therefore, a surplus of rural population and a large labour surplus in spite of the fact that Egypt has the most intensive system of agriculture in the world.

When the area per head is interpreted in terms of cash the income of the individual peasant is incredibly small, notwithstanding the fact that the output of the land is the highest in the world in maize and cotton, and is as high as that of Britain in wheat.[3] A survey carried out in 1938 with a view to determining the gross output from agriculture indicated that the figure per head of the population was £E.5·012 in upper and £E.6·275 in lower Egypt.[4] Another estimate puts the average total annual income of an agricultural family of 5–6 persons at £E.20–30.[5] This is in the case of families that own their small plots of land. A fellah who rents land has a worse deal. He has to pay exorbitant rents which range from £E.6 to £E.22 per feddan,[6] and has to pay taxes and high rates of interest to money lenders. With regard to agricultural labourers their lot is the same if not worse. These live on wages of 2–3 piastres a day (1 piastre equals 2½d), and they can only find employment for a period of 6–8 months in the year. Wages rose to about 6 piastres a day during the war, but this rise was offset by the corresponding rise in the cost of living.[7] This state of affairs has naturally led to an appallingly low standard of living which no visitor to Egypt can fail to notice. The fellah is not only badly housed, underfed and under-clothed, but he suffers from diseases which undermine his health and his outlook on life. The incidence of bilharzia in rural areas is between 45 and 75 per cent.[8] Pellagra, rickets and night blindness are very common.[9] 90 per cent suffer

[1] *Ibid.*   [2] *Ibid.*, p. 32.
[3] *Ibid.*, p. 29.
[4] *Issawi*, pp. 47–48.
[5] A. Bonné, *op. cit.*, p. 29; also Simaika in *Engineering Magazine*, Cairo, May, 1948.
[6] *Ibid.*, also A. Bonné, *State and Economics in the Middle East*, London, 1948, p. 129.
[7] Doreen Warriner, *op. cit.*, p. 38.
[8] *Ibid.*, p. 42.
[9] *Ibid.*, p. 39.

from trachoma, 50 per cent from anklystoma, 50 per cent from worm diseases, and over 300,000 from tuberculosis.[1]

Agricultural machinery is not used on any large scale in Egypt; but should such machinery be used the situation would be desperate. A survey by Dr. W. Cleland shows that between one-fifth and one-half of the present labour force could maintain the present standards of production. Taking half as a basis, labour could be cut by two million and farm population by 5 million. If machinery is introduced only 10 per cent of the present labour force could do the work.[2]

Egypt, therefore, has a problem which demands immediate solution, from every thinking statesman and every social reformer. It is a problem about which the Western Powers, which are interested in the political and social stability in Egypt and the Middle East, show their concern.[3] What are the remedies? Birth control, reclamation of land from lakes and desert, industrialization, redistribution of land, and emigration have been suggested as possible remedies by those who investigated Egypt's social and economic problems. This book is not the place to discuss all the possibilities of solving Egypt's population problem. Only those possible solutions which are relevant to the dispute over the Sudan will be dealt with here.

The first is the possibility of relieving Egypt of her surplus population by emigration. The Sudan and Iraq have been suggested by almost every person who has made a study of the problem, or who is in one way or another associated with it.[4] As soon as the population problem became clear to Egyptian statesmen after the Census of 1927, they introduced the question of Egyptian immigration into the Sudan, for the first time in the history of the dispute, into the negotiations with Britain for the settlement of the Sudan question. We have seen how Egyptian insistence on unrestricted Egyptian immigration into the Sudan was partly responsible for the failure of the Nahas-Henderson negotiations of 1930.[5] Nahas Pasha and his colleagues brought the question up

---

[1] A. Bonné. The Economic Development of the Middle East. op. cit., p. 31.
[2] Doreen Warriner, op. cit., p. 33.   [3] The Times, 19th January, 1949.
[4] Hurst, Black and Simaika, p. 14; Issawi, p. 196; Abbas Hilmi op. cit., pp. 28–29; Doreen Warriner, op. cit., pp. 50–51.
[5] See p. 67.

again in 1936 and succeeded in obtaining British agreement to unrestricted immigration, except on grounds of public health and public order.

But the difficulty in the way of Egyptian emigration is the fellah's own apathy and ignorance of the world around him. The ill health of the fellaheen 'dulls their minds and diminishes their ambition to a sufficient extent, so that they have no courage to face an adventure into some unknown area where they might improve their conditions'.[1] This is born out by the fact that no immigration in any appreciable quantity has taken place into the Sudan since the signing of the 1936 Treaty. But it may be that with some organization and encouragement the Egyptians may be persuaded to migrate to the Sudan. Whether or not the Sudanese will welcome an influx of Egyptian peasants remains to be seen. The Sudan to-day is in need of labour and is capable of absorbing immigrants. Its labour needs are met by Nigerians and French Equatorial Africans. The writer recollects the opposition which his colleagues on the Advisory Council for the Northern Sudan, who were also members of the Independence Front, put up in private discussions against Egyptian immigration. They feared that if the Egyptians migrated to the Sudan in big numbers they would form Egypt's 'fifth column' in the Sudan and resist the independence movement. Egyptian immigration, however, putting political considerations aside, is much more advantageous to the Sudan than immigration from West Africa. There is enough evidence to show that immigrants from Egypt can be quickly assimilated while West Africans who settled in the Sudan live as separate communities especially in places where the population is of Arab origin.

Emigration to the Sudan as a solution to Egypt's problem of over-population may turn out to be a real one or it may be an illusion. But the fact remains that the question of unrestricted immigration played a prominent part in the dispute and may still be a major issue.

The problem of over-population leads Egypt to concentrate upon industrialization as a possible remedy and the Sudan therefore assumes a further interest to her as a market for her

---

[1] W. Cleland, *The Population Problem in Egypt*, Lancaster, Pennsylvania, 1936, p. 87.

manufactures. The success of Egyptian industries depends, amongst other things, on the purchasing power of the Egyptian peasant. If this is not increased, and there are no indications that it will be, and since Egypt cannot under normal conditions compete with the big industrial countries, a Sudan market controlled by Egypt would help to keep her industries going.

One of Egypt's main industries is the cotton textile industry, and as the 8 million Sudanese wear cotton clothes all the year round, there is a big demand for cheap cotton piece goods in the Sudan. Practically the whole supply of these goods used to come from Japan before the second world war. Egypt could not compete with Japan in spite of the fact that the 1899 Agreement provides that no import duties should be collected on goods coming from Egypt. Japan exported to the Sudan in 1939 £E.799,000 worth of cotton piece goods against Egypt's £E.10,000.[1] Egypt's exports rose to £E.63,000 in 1941[2] and jumped to £E.962,912 in 1947[3]. If Egypt could control the Sudan market she would certainly protect her interests even if Japan or another country were to compete with her.

Another example may be taken from the sugar industry. The Sudan Government, which has a sugar monopoly, used to import its supply from Egypt. The value of sugar imported from Egypt in 1941 was £E.1,077,000[4]. After this year the sugar producers in Egypt disagreed over the prices and the Sudan Government began to import from somewhere else. The value of sugar imports began to dwindle until it came down to 9,242 Egyptian pounds in 1947.[5] If Egypt had been responsible for the administration of the Sudan the story might have been different.[6]

Finally, brief reference must be made in this short analysis to the employment of Egyptian capital in the Sudan. So far, all the capital necessary for the development of the Sudan has been raised in Britain.[7] Egyptian capital that was used for development in the Sudan was in the form of loans without interest.

[1] *Review of Commercial Conditions*, p. 19.
[2] *Ibid.*, p. 22.
[3] Annual Report, 1947, p. 59.
[4] *Review of Commercial Conditions*, p. 22.
[5] Annual Report, 1947, p. 59.
[6] For Egypt's trade with the Sudan see also p. 97.
[7] See below p. 95.

Egypt advanced to the Sudan Government over 4 million pounds (1901-1909) for capital expenditure on such works as railway buildings and the construction of Port Sudan.[1] But Egyptian capitalists look upon the Sudan as a place for investment which must not be used as such exclusively by the British. 'We consider', wrote the ex-Khedive (Abbas II), 'that the right of Egyptians to participate in the development of the country (the Sudan) must be asserted, and full equality in the opportunities of investment with those enjoyed by the British capitalists should be claimed and accorded.'[2]

[1] Toynbee, p. 240.
[2] Abbas Hilmi, *op. cit.*, p. 29.

CHAPTER IX

BRITISH INTERESTS IN THE SUDAN

GREAT BRITAIN'S position with regard to the Sudan in the latest phase of the dispute must also be seen against the background of her interests there.

Her first interest, but not necessarily the most important one, is the investment of capital. The Sudan borrowed over 15 million pounds from British investors for the construction of the Sennar dam, the digging of the main canals, and the building of some of the railways. The annual service of the debt required £E.907,002 in 1932, much the same amount until 1938, and very nearly one million pounds sterling until 1944. A part of the debt was redeemed in 1939, but a further loan of 2 million pounds at a lower rate of interest was raised in England to make the redemption possible. But the Sudan will continue to pay a gradually decreasing debt service until 1974.[1]

In addition to the capital investment, the management of the Gezira scheme was entrusted to a British Company, the Sudan Plantations Syndicate, for the supervision of cultivation, the ginning, and the marketing of cotton. The company in return was allotted about 20 per cent of the net proceeds of the cotton. Its concession, however, was terminated on 30th June, 1950 and a board, appointed by the Sudan Government, took over the management of the scheme. Another British firm which has sunk capital in the country is the Sudan Light and Power Company which has been supplying water and electricity to several Sudanese towns. There is also a firm working a small gold mine in Gebeit. This is the only firm to sink capital out of a number of firms which were given concessions early in the century to investigate the mining possibilities and which all met the same disillusion as Mohammed Ali Pasha.

These financial investments constituted a British interest which was at one time used as an argument against the change in the

[1] MacMichael, p. 230.

status of the Sudan which Egypt was demanding. Mr. Lloyd George, in a speech on 28th February, 1922, the day on which the independence of Egypt was declared, 'ruled out any change in the status of the Sudan which would "in the slightest degree diminish the security" for the British capital which had already been vested in Sudanese development'.[1] The importance of this investment, however, must not be over-exaggerated in the later stages of the dispute because, unless the Sudan incurs further loans, the importance of the country as a field of investment seems to be diminishing. The first British firm, for over 20 years, to be given permission to invest capital is the Sudan Meat Products Ltd., incorporated in the Sudan on 21st November, 1949, with a nominal capital of £E.400,000. The capital was provided by Liebigs Extract of Meat Company Ltd., London, but the arrangement was made that as soon as the factory was ready to go into production the Company would invite Sudanese participation up to 30 per cent.[2]

Britain is also interested in Sudan cotton. This interest made some British members of parliament ask that the loans should be conditional on the sale of Sudanese cotton to Britain.[3] No such condition was accepted but the Sudan cotton, especially the long staple Sakel variety, which is grown in the Gezira, went mainly to Great Britain and to India when it was British. In the four years which preceded the second world war Britain bought 61 per cent of the Sakel crop and British India bought 23 per cent.[4] Beginning with the 1942–3 yield till one year after the end of the war the entire crops of both Sakel and American types were sold to the Ministry of Supply.[5] In 1946 and 1947 Great Britain bought 54·3 per cent and 58·5 per cent respectively of the total export of Sudan Sakel.[6] When compared with countries which produce cotton within the British Empire, the Sudan ranks third. The first two are India (including Pakistan) and Uganda, but on two occasions in recent years the Sudan production exceeded that of

[1] Toynbee, p. 246.
[2] Sudan Assembly, Second Session, Vol. 3, pp. 17–18. Statement by the Under-Secretary for Economics and Trade on 25th March, 1950.
[3] Correspondence respecting the Gezira Irrigation Project, 1924. Cmd. 2171.
[4] Tothill, *op. cit.*, p. 336.
[5] *Review of Commercial Conditions*, p. 15.
[6] *Foreign Trade Report*, p. 108.

Uganda.[1] It should be noted however, that Sudan cotton is of a much higher quality than that of India and Uganda. When compared with world production Sudan yields are still small. They averaged about 1 per cent of world production during 1936-39.[2] Nevertheless they are gradually occupying an important place in the British cotton trade. Britain's cotton imports from Egypt in 1946 were nearly 1.5 million kantars.[3] The Sudan's importance as a cotton producing country will increase with the expansion of agriculture in the Gezira, the prospects of which were discussed in Chapter VII.

The general trade relations between Britain and the Sudan must also be taken into consideration. It is not possible to give a detailed analysis here but the following percentages will throw light on the situation. Percentages of trade with Egypt are also given below for comparison.

Percentages of Sudan Imports from Great Britain and Egypt[4]

	1938	1939	1945	1946	1947	1948
United Kingdom	26·2	27·7	12·7	23·9	24·0	30·4
Egypt	23·0	28·3	16·9	18·8	21·6	21·4

Percentages of Sudan Exports to Great Britain and Egypt[5]

	1938	1939	1945	1946	1947	1948
United Kingdom	47·1	47·5	42·6	36·5	39·6	61·8
Egypt	13·1	9·0	23·6	18·4	17·8	13·7

These percentages show the strength of trade relations between the Sudan and the disputants. It will be noticed that of the two Co-domini, Britain, has the stronger trade relations with the Sudan.

The British also have a strategic interest in the Sudan. The interests of Britain in the Suez Canal and in the Middle East in

[1] Tothill, *op. cit.*, p. 336.
[2] *Ibid.*
[3] *Overseas Economic Survey: Egypt,* His Majesty's Stationery Office, 1947, p. 77.
[4] 1938 and 1939 percentages from *Review of Commercial Conditions,* p. 11; 1945–47 from *Foreign Trade Report,* p. 6; 1948 percentages from *Foreign Trade and Internal Statistics,* January, 1949, Department of Economics and Trade, p. 17.
[5] *Ibid.*

general are well known. If Britain removes her forces from Egypt, her strategic interests make it imperative for her to station them somewhere else in the Middle East. The Sudan is regarded by experts as a possible alternative. 'Control of the Sudan', it has been said, 'has always been of considerable strategic importance to the British Empire, and as British authority in Egypt diminishes, so does this importance increase'.[1] The same opinion is expressed in the official story of the conquest of Italian East Africa in these terms: 'If the Anglo-Egyptian Sudan had gone, the supply lines of the Middle East up to the Red Sea and across Africa from Takoradi to Khartoum would have gone too. Egypt itself would have become untenable. There would have been, in fact, no front in the Middle East. The wasp-waist of the British Empire would have been severed by pincers of which the northern arm would have been Graziani's armies advancing from Libya, and the southern arm would have been the Italian armies advancing from East Africa.'[2]

The Sudan made valuable contributions to the allied cause during the second world war. The Sudan Defence Force managed to bluff the Italians and prevent them from marching into the Sudan until the British and Indian forces arrived and started their successful Ethiopian and Eritrean Campaigns. The Sudan Railways and steamers rendered a valuable and efficient service and the country supplied the Middle East Armies with appreciable amounts of foodstuffs. The Sudan Government also made gifts in cash amounting to £300,000 to the British and Indian Governments. These and other Sudanese services during the war were appreciated by the British Government which later gave the Sudan £2,000,000 in recognition of the contributions towards the allied cause.

There is also the British interest in air communications. The busy Khartoum aerodrome has become not only an important link in the Cape-to-Cairo air line, but indeed the important African air junction through which services pass to the north, connecting with United Kingdom and Far Eastern services,

[1] The Royal Institute of International Affairs: *Political and Strategic Interests of the United Kingdom*, Oxford, 1940, pp. 118–119.
[2] *The Abyssinian Campaigns*, His Majesty's Stationery Office, London, 1942, p. 12.

southwards to east, central and South Africa, westwards to the west coast of Africa and to the east to Eritrea, Ethiopia and Aden.[1] 6,922 planes landed in the Sudan in 1947,[2] and Khartoum airport was extremely important to the Royal Air Force during the last war, and also to the United States Air Force. The Americans, indeed, had their own aerodrome at Wadi Seidna, some twelve miles north of Khartoum.

The Sudan also provides a field of employment for Englishmen who prefer to seek a career abroad. There were just under 1,000 posts occupied by non-Sudanese in 1948.[3] Just under 700 of these were Division I posts and were, with few exceptions, held by Britons. The remainder were Division II posts and were mostly held by British nationals.

Finally, there is what might be called the 'paternal' interest. In the British Government statements, and in the eyes of many Englishmen who either served in the Sudan or took general interest in it, the country is regarded as an adopted son. But this adopted son, the British argue, is not like 'France's adopted daughter', Egypt, who, like many adopted daughters, was loved chiefly for the sake of her fortune. On 7th October, 1924, Mr. Ramsay MacDonald wrote, 'Since going there, they (the British Government) have contracted heavy moral obligations by the creation of a good system of administration; they cannot allow that to be destroyed; they regard their responsibilities as a trust for the Sudan people; there can be no question of their abandoning the Sudan until their work is done.'[4] Turning to 20th November, 1950, we find Mr. Ernest Bevin telling the House of Commons, 'The Sudan is a really remarkable development and is an example to the world of what can be done in such territories and we would do nothing at all to set it back and leave the people to the tender mercy of others.' The British Government's attitude has thus remained constant. To any one who has lived long in the country, the attitude of the Sudan Government would appear even more pronounced. If the adopted son, in his moderate moods, asks for

---

[1] *Review of Commercial Conditions*, p. 7.
[2] *Foreign Trade Report*, p. 181.
[3] Sudan Government, *Report of the Committee on the Administration of the Civil Service*, Khartoum, 1948, Appendix 2.
[4] Cmd. 2269, 1924, *op. cit.*, p. 4.

a key to the front door, or if in his less temperate moods he says
with William Harbutt Dawson, 'The most efficient of alien
governments can never be an altogether satisfactory substitute for
the least efficient of native administrations,'[1] he is told he will be
regarded as an adult 'when the time comes.'

---

[1] William Harbutt Dawson, *The British Occupation of Egypt*, 1879–1883, in Ward
and Gooch, *op. cit.*, Vol III, p. 165.

PART THREE

THE LATER PHASES
OF THE DISPUTE

CHAPTER X

THE EMERGENCE OF THE SUDANESE

I HAVE said that Turkey, ceased to be a party in the dispute, in actual practice, after the declaration of the British protectorate over Egypt in 1915, and, in international law, after the signature of the Treaty of Lausanne in 1923. A new third party, however, appeared, more vigorous in character and with a much stronger title. This party was the Sudanese. But they did not appear on the scene until after the second world war. Although they were not admitted to take part in the negotiations for the revision of the 1936 Treaty, in 1945, the year which marked the opening of the latest phases, their right to self-government and self-determination was, as we shall see, unequivocally recognized by Great Britain from the very beginning of the negotiations and under pressure from the Security Council, this was eventually admitted by the Egyptian Prime Minister.

It is important, if the latest phases are to be fully appreciated, to describe the rise of this third party. Why were the Sudanese not a party in the dispute from the early stages? How did they come to be a party? Are they sufficiently qualified to shoulder the responsibilities of self-government and independence? These are the questions which this chapter will attempt to answer.

There were various reasons why the Sudanese were out of the picture in the early stages. Their leaders, unlike chiefs in other parts of Africa, never established diplomatic relations with any European power, or asked for terms before they were overwhelmed by the forces of Kitchener in the battle of Omdurman in September, 1898. The Khalifa and the generals who survived that battle with him continued the struggle for over a year. When they were convinced of their utter defeat, they spread their praying mats and waited for the bullets that finished them in the battle of Um Debeikrat in November, 1899. The Sudanese were, therefore, in the eyes of Great Britain, Egypt and the world in general, a vanquished people who, by the practice of those days, were not entitled to a say in the settlement of their future.

From within, the people went through thirteen years of native rule during which they experienced incessant fighting, recurrent famines, serious outbreaks of epidemic diseases, and a form of oppression worse than that which had driven them to rally behind the banner of the Mahdi. They emerged as weary, impoverished, displaced fragments of tribes who wanted nothing more than a settled life in which they could find peace and security.

But the forty-seven years which lapsed between the beginning of the new regime and the opening of the latest phases of the dispute gradually brought about modifications in world political thought, introduced new ideals in imperial policies, and saw many changes in the Sudan. In the international field the new ideals of self-government and self-determination adopted by the Allies during the first world war and embodied in the League of Nations Covenant, were carried further in the Charter of the United Nations. This laid down as one of its purposes the development of 'friendly relations among nations based on respect for the principle of equal rights and self-determination of peoples,'[1] and which had one of its basic objectives the 'progressive development towards self-government or independence as may be appropriate to the particular circumstances of each territory and its peoples'.[2]

The changes which took place within the Sudan were not less spectacular. The organized system of administration and the agricultural development of the Gezira produced remarkable results. They brought about economic prosperity which, in its turn, rendered possible the spread of education. When the Sudanese were educated in sufficient numbers, they were able to man the civil service, they became politically conscious, and the country began to make constitutional progress. A brief survey of these developments will show the degree of the strength won by the Sudanese as a third party and to what extent their claims to take over the government of their country are justified.

[1] Article 1 (2).
[2] Article 76 (b).

In the economic sphere the total revenue, which rose from £E.126,569 in 1899[1] to just over £E.1½ million in 1913,[2] the first year in which the Sudan balanced its budget, reached over £E.10 million in 1947.[3] The increase of revenue was rendered possible by the production of cotton in the Gezira. When world cotton prices went up, the revenue of the Sudan exceeded £E.18½ million in 1949,[4] and the estimated revenue for the eighteen months between January, 1950, and June, 1951, was £E.36¾ million.[5] The Sudan Government had a total reserve of just under £E.13½ million in 1947.[6] The figure was £E.13·1 million in 1948 and the surplus of revenue over the expenditure at the end of 1949 which amounted to £E.7·1 million was added to the reserves.[7] The figures of foreign trade also showed remarkable increases. The total value rose from just over a million in 1902[8] to a little short of £E.32 million in 1947,[9] and £E.51½ million in 1949 with a favourable balance of trade of some £E.3½ million.[10]

The financial position rendered possible the development of the educational service. The total expenditure upon government schools and upon the Gordon Memorial College amounted to £E.1·1 million in 1947. This included current and capital expenditure.[11] The Legislative Assembly approved an educational development plan which will raise the recurrent expenditure to over £E.1 million in 1951 and to £E.1½ million in 1956. The estimated capital expenditure for the plan is £E.2½ million.[12] The Sudan secondary schools have for the last ten years been taking the Cambridge School Certificate,[13] and Gordon Memorial

---

[1] MacMichael, p. 78.
[2] *Ibid.*, p. 91.
[3] Annual Report, 1947, p. 26.
[4] Sudan Assembly, Second Session, Vol. II, 15th March, 1950, p. 2.
[5] *Ibid.*, pp. 7 and 13.
[6] Annual Report, 1947, p. 26.
[7] Sudan Assembly, Second Session, Vol. 2, 15th March, 1950, p. 5.
[8] MacMichael, p. 91.
[9] Annual Report, 1947, p. 11.
[10] Sudan Assembly, Second Session. Vol. 2, 15th March, 1950, p. 4.
[11] *Foreign Trade Report*, p. 187.
[12] Sudan Ministry of Education, *Summary of the amended Educational Plan* (Arabic) 1949-1956, p. 7.
[13] The standard of secondary education prior to the introduction of the Cambridge School Certificate was considered to be near that of the English Schools. See Report of a Commission of Inspection on the Gordon Memorial College, Khartoum, 1929, p. 11.

College students have lately begun to work for London external general degrees in arts and sciences.[1] In addition to these local educational facilities, an increasing number of Sudanese have been attending university and other courses abroad. The first missions were sent to the American University of Beirut between 1925 and 1933. From 1937 onwards the Sudan Government decided to send educational missions to England. The number of Sudanese taking various degree, diploma and other courses in 1950 was over a hundred. About the same number attends university courses in Egypt, and the Egyptian Government sent a few Sudanese graduates of Egyptian universities for further courses in Paris.

Education helped the Sudan to avoid the problem, once faced by East Africa, of importing civil servants in large numbers from outside. 'Of the total classified staff in the civil service', wrote the Governor-General in his annual report for 1947, 'British personnel accounted for 10·99 per cent, Egyptians for 3·70 per cent, and other non-Sudanese 0.34 per cent. Sudanese holders of classified posts . . . form 84·97 per cent of the total as compared with 50·9 per cent in 1930 and 36·8 per cent in 1920.'[2] All the senior posts were, until 1936, occupied by British and other foreign civil servants. From this year the Sudanese began to hold senior posts. 126 such posts were occupied by Sudanese in 1948 against 694 occupied by non-Sudanese.[3] The Sudanization of the civil service is progressing according to a plan worked out by a Committee which was appointed by the Governor-General in 1946. The Committee reported in 1948 and, according to its plans, 62.2 per cent of the posts previously held by non-Sudanese are to be Sudanized by 1962.[4] The recruitment of non-Sudanese on

---

[1] *Editor's Note*. It may be useful to remind readers who may not be familiar with the history of the Sudan that, largely owing to the vision of Lord Kitchener and the hold of General Gordon upon the affection of his country, the Sudan Government was able to make a start with education that was exceptionally early for a government in a newly occupied Moslem country. Subscriptions were being raised in England before the end of 1898; the first Director of Education was appointed by 1900, and the school opened in 1902. From little more than a primary school, it developed in 1950 into a University College taking London degrees.

[2] Annual Report, 1947, pp. 12–13.

[3] Sudan Government, *Report of the Committee on the Sudanization of the Civil Service*, Khartoum, 1948. Appendix 2.

[4] *Ibid.* Appendix 5.

pensionable service was suspended in 1947 as a part of the Sudanization policy. The new arrangement has been to take all foreign
civil servants on short or long term contracts ranging from seven
to twenty years.

Financial independence and the Sudanization of the civil service are not, of course, enough to make the country ready for self-
government, or independence if it is not to be ruled by a despot
or by the heads of the civil service. Political maturity and constitutional progress are just as essential.

In the political field the first signs of national consciousness
began to show themselves among the educated class after the first
world war. A number of societies and leagues were founded
between 1921 and 1924 claiming either independence for the
Sudan or a form of unity with Egypt, but, with the exception of
the White Flag League, which stood for the freedom and unity of
the Nile Valley and which was very active in 1924, they were
extremely nebulous and died away afterwards.[1] These societies
lodged protests and staged demonstrations in the big towns, and,
between June and November, 1924, there were riots in which the
civil population took part. There were, in addition, mutinies by
some units of Sudanese troops which formed part of the Egyptian
Army in the Sudan. One of these mutinies was serious and in the
course of its suppression both English and Sudanese blood was
shed.[2] 'The even tenor of administrative progress', wrote the
Governor-General in his 1924 report, 'and peaceful development
chronicled in these reports from year to year was rudely interrupted during the latter half of 1924 by political agitation which
threatened public security for the first time in the history of the
Condominium'.[3]

Strict measures were taken by the Government and, because
the agitation was nothing but a sign of a new political consciousness which had not taken any deep root, all was quiet by the end
of 1924.

The first occasion on which the political feelings of the educated
Sudanese were aroused on a wide scale after the 1924 incidents

[1] A note on these societies was prepared for the writer by the Civil Secretary's
Office, Khartoum.
[2] MacMichael, pp. 159–60.
[3] Annual Report, 1925, p. 4.

was in 1931. The occasion was not a political one, but once collective action started over what might be called a trade union
grievance, it was easily diverted into political channels. In that
year the Sudan Government decided to reduce the starting rate
of pay of employees newly 'graduating' from Gordon College from
eight pounds a month to five and a half. No reduction in the
starting rates of British officials was made.[1] This caused an out-
burst of ill-feeling amongst the pupils and the graduates of
Gordon College. The pupils went on strike, and the efforts of
parents and religious leaders to make them return to work were
of no avail. The graduates called a general meeting in their club
and elected a committee of ten members to take up the matter
with the Government. After prolonged negotiations the grievance
was partly redressed and the question was settled.[2] This incident
had two effects on the educated Sudanese. In the first place,
because it was a tangible injustice, it left a real sense of grievance
which was not felt in 1924. Had the reduction in starting rates of
pay, necessitated, it was argued, by a financial crisis, been
universal there would not have been a feeling that an injustice
was done. In the second place it brought home to the graduates
of Gordon College the importance of organizing themselves, not
only for the protection of their interests, but also for political
purposes.

No special organization came into being immediately, but as
soon as the question of the Sudan came up for discussion in the
1936 negotiations, the course of which 'was watched by the more
instructed elements of the population with keen interest and some
apprehensions',[3] the graduates of Gordon College and other
schools began to feel strongly the need for organizing themselves.
The idea matured towards the end of 1937, and the 'Graduates
General Congress' was formed. The membership of Congress was
confined to the graduates of all schools at the beginning, but was
later extended to all literate Sudanese. The motive behind the
organization was political, but, since almost all the graduates of
Gordon College and most of the graduates of the lower grade

---

[1] Reductions however in the salaries of civil servants included the British civil
servant.

[2] E. Atiyah: *An Arab Tells His Story*, London, 1946, pp. 163–9.

[3] Annual Report, 1936, p. 7.

schools were civil servants, congress men, in order to secure permission from the Government to set up the organization, worded their aim in very vague terms. It was 'to serve the public interest of the country and of the graduates'. When the Civil Secretary of the Sudan Government approved the formation of Congress he did so on the understanding that it was not political and that it represented only the views of its members.[1]

The activities of Congress in the first years were restricted mainly to the encouragement of private schools, but its activities in the political field were not long delayed. It unveiled its political intentions when its president submitted a memorandum to the Governor-General, on 3rd April, 1942, on behalf of the Sudanese people. The memorandum contained twelve demands the most important of which were 'the issue, on the first possible opportunity, by the British and Egyptian Governments, of a joint declaration guaranteeing the Sudan, in its geographical boundaries, the right of self-determination directly after the war'; the promulgation of a Sudanese nationality law; and the creation of a representative body to approve the budget and the ordinances.

The reply of the Civil Secretary on behalf of the Governor-General was a complete rebuff. It came as a surprise to many Sudanese who had intimate knowledge of the deep sympathy which was felt by Sir Douglas Newbold, the Civil Secretary, and Sir Hubert Huddleston, the Governor-General, for the aspirations of the Sudanese. They returned the memorandum and refused to enter into any discussion of a political nature.[2] Further communications and discussions of a private nature between the president of the Congress and the Civil Secretary followed, but, although the Civil Secretary assured the president of the Government's goodwill,[3] no favourable official reply was made.[4] Some Congress

[1] *Civil Secretary to President of Congress*, 22nd May, 1938.
[2] *Civil Secretary to President of Congress*, No. CS/10. c.7 dated 29th April, 1942.
[3] President of Congress to the Governor-General through the Civil Secretary dated 12th May, 1942; also D. Newbold (Civil Secretary) to Ibrahim Ahmed (President of Congress) dated 17th July, 1942; also I. Ahmed to D. Newbold dated 23rd July, 1942.
[4] *Editor's Note*. I think it is only fair to Sir Douglas Newbold to add to the account given here a reminder that at this time almost his whole time and energy were taken up with the war at a most critical phase. The next year he died as a result of overwork and the strain of this period. Further light will be thrown upon this event by a forthcoming book in this Series upon the life and letters of Sir Douglas Newbold.

members were prepared to accept the assurances given privately, but others refused to accept anything less than a formal acceptance of the demands embodied in the memorandum. The result was a split in Congress and the formation of parties within its framework. Those who trusted the Civil Secretary formed independence parties, chief of which was the Umma Party, and the others, who regarded the unsympathetic official attitude of the Sudan Government as representing the attitude of the British Government, thought that the best way of achieving their goal was to adopt a policy which might gain them the support of Egypt. They formed 'unity' parties, chief of which was the Ashigga Party. When the latter parties won a majority of seats in a Congress election which followed the split, they passed a resolution, in the name of Congress, determining the goal of the Sudanese to be 'the setting up of a Sudanese democratic government in union with Egypt under the Egyptian Crown,'[1] and sent it to the Governor-General, requesting him to communicate it to the British and Egyptian Governments.

The competition between the two groups of parties within Congress, and their desire to gain popular support, made leaders seek the help of the two rival religious leaders. The independence group resorted to Sir Sayid Abdel Rahman El Mahdi Pasha, the posthumous son of the Mahdi, who later became the virtual leader of the 'Independence Front', and the unity parties went to Sir Sayid Ali El Mirghani Pasha who gave them his blessing. The reason for the rivalry between the two religious leaders was that El Mirghani, whose father had been persecuted throughout the Mahdia regime, accused El Mahdi of ambitions to become the monarch of an independent Sudan. He therefore associated the independence movement with a Mahdist monarchy and preferred to see the Sudan under the crown of Farouk rather than risk the possibility of its assumption by Abdel Rahman.[2]

When the British Government agreed late in 1945 to the request of the Egyptian Government to start negotiations for the revision of the 1936 Treaty, some independent members of Congress, who were anxious to see all parties united during the

---

[1] *Sawt El Sudan* (a Khartoum daily paper), 8th April, 1945.
[2] For further discussion of this subject see below p. 129.

negotiations which they feared might result in a settlement unfavourable to Sudanese aspirations, made efforts to bridge the gap between the independence and unity groups. They worked out a formula which was accepted by both sides, and a delegation consisting of representatives of all parties was dispatched to Cairo to acquaint the negotiators with the demands of the Sudanese. The formula ran as follows:—

1. 'The setting up of a free Sudanese democratic government in union with Egypt and in alliance with Great Britain.' The free Sudanese Government chooses the form of union with Egypt, and in the light of that union decides the type of alliance with Britain.

2. Asking for the appointment of a joint committee, half of the members of which should be appointed by the Co-domini and the other half by Congress from amongst the enlightened class of Sudanese, to make proposals for handing the government over to the Sudanese in the shortest possible time.

3. The guaranteeing of the freedom of the press, public meetings, and the freedom of movement and trade.[1]

When the Sudanese delegation arrived in Cairo, its members started talks with Egyptian politicians of all types who insisted that the Sudanese should accept an undefined permanent unity under the Egyptian Crown. This the independence members refused to accept, and they parted company with their colleagues who represented the unity parties and who preferred to remain in Cairo.

Ever since that date the two groups of Sudanese parties have opposed each other and sent separate delegations, to London when Sidky Pasha travelled to negotiate with Mr. Bevin, and to Lake Success when Nokrashi Pasha took the dispute to the Security Council.

While the political parties were engaged in their struggle to influence the negotiations, members of the Advisory Council for the Northern Sudan, which was formed in 1944, asked the Governor-General for an assurance that their future would not be settled before they were consulted. This was given on 3rd November, 1945. The Governor-General assured the Council of 'the Government's firm intention to consult the people of the Sudan

---

[1] *Sawt El Sudan*, 13th October, 1945, and 20th March, 1946.

regarding the future of their country.'[1] But the anxiety of the Sudanese increased to such an extent that Mr. Bevin found it necessary to make a statement in the House of Commons on 26th March, 1946. He said in that statement, 'His Majesty's Government look forward to the day when the Sudanese will be able finally to decide their political future for themselves.' He also added that the object of the administration in the Sudan was to establish organs of self-government as a first step towards eventual independence, and assured the Sudanese that no change would be made in the status of the Sudan as a result of treaty revision until they were consulted through constitutional channels. Mr. Bevin's assurances were again repeated by the Governor-General to the Advisory Council on 17th April, 1946.[2]

Developments in the constitutional field did not lag far behind the political advancement of the Sudanese. In the sphere of local government they began to shoulder responsibilities as early as 1922. By 1947 nearly all the rural areas had their local authorities and all the five municipalities and over ten townships had their warrants and councils. The Sudan Government, which was giving much attention to the development of local government, invited Dr. Marshall, the treasurer of Coventry, in 1948, 'to enquire into and report on the policy and practice of local government and to make recommendations on any matter arising from the enquiry'. Dr. Marshall's report, which was published by the Sudan Government in 1949, endorsed the government's policy of following the English model, and the recommendations made in the report on the future development of the system have been accepted by the Executive Council and the Legislative Assembly.

The Sudanese did not begin to participate in the sphere of central government until 1944. In this year the Governor-General, with the consent of Great Britain and Egypt, set up an advisory council for the Northern Sudan. This council, as its name indicates, was purely advisory to the Governor-General; but the experience gained in it justified a further step towards the association of the Sudanese more closely with the government of

---

[1] *Proceedings of the Advisory Council for the Northern Sudan*, 4th Session, 3rd November, 1945.
[2] *Ibid.*, 5th Session, 17th April, 1946.

their country. Plans for the second step were almost ready when the dispute was being debated in the Security Council in August, 1947, but they were not put into effect until December, 1948. The reason for the delay was the disagreement between Great Britain and Egypt over the manner in which the Sudanese should be associated with the government of their country and over the extent of Egyptian participation in training them for self-government.

The step, which was taken without Egyptian consent, involved the creation of an Executive Council and a Legislative Assembly. The Council is responsible for the executive and administrative functions of the government and the Assembly for the passing of legislation except in respect of four reserved matters and the three special matters. The reserved matters were:—

(a) The provisions of the ordinance creating the Council and the Assembly.

(b) The relations between the Sudan Government and the British and Egyptian Governments.

(c) The relations between the Sudan Government and foreign governments.

(d) The nationality of the Sudanese.

The special matters were the defence of the Sudan, coinage and currency, and the status of religious or racial minorities. The Assembly has no legislative powers in respect of the reserved matters but private members may initiate legislation affecting the special matters with the prior consent of the Executive Council.[1]

The ordinance creating the Council and the assembly laid down that at least half the members of the Council should be Sudanese, and when the Council was formed six of its twelve seats were filled by Sudanese, three of whom were given the portfolios of agriculture, education and health.[2] It also laid down that all the elected and nominated members of the Assembly should be Sudanese. Of the 91 members of this first Legislative Assembly, 85 were Sudanese: ten of these were directly elected, 58 elected by electoral colleges, and 33 nominated by the Governor-General. The

[1] *The Executive Council and Legislative Assembly Ordinance*, Sudan Government Gazette No. 791 dated 19th June, 1948, Chapter V, Sections 54 and 55.

[2] When a British member without portfolio resigned his seat in June, 1950, it was filled by a Sudanese.

remaining six were the British members of the Executive Council.

The Executive Council and the Legislative Assembly were intended to develop into a cabinet and a chamber of deputies. The main respect in which the constitutional developments of 1948 fall short of a parliamentary system is that the Executive Council is appointed by the Governor-General and is responsible to him. The Governor-General also 'may, for reasons to be recorded in the record of the proceedings of the Council, and to be notified forthwith to the two Governments aforesaid, veto any decision made by the majority of the Council and substitute his own decision therefore. . . .'[1] This was because the 1899 Agreement, which vested the supreme civil and military command in the Governor-General, remained, at least in theory, unchanged. These supreme powers were, however, curtailed by the Executive Council and Legislative Assembly Ordinance, 1948. Whereas previously to the promulgation of this ordinance the Governor-General was the sole ultimate authority for making laws and was only required by the terms of the Agreement to notify the British and the Egyptian Governments of all the laws which he should make by proclamation, he cannot, by the provisions of the Executive Council and Legislative Assembly Ordinance 1948, give his assent to a bill over which the Executive Council and Legislative Assembly fail to reach agreement, without reference to his Majesty's Government in the United Kingdon and the Royal Egyptian Government.[2]

It is clear from the above that the Sudanese have not emerged in the dispute as a party which has the legal international status exercised by Britain and Egypt or by Turkey in the early stages. But it should be equally clear that their advancement in the educational, economic, political and constitutional spheres, added to their rights to self-government and self-determination recognized by the United Nations Charter, give them an unquestioned moral right to be the first party in the dispute in the latest stages which it has reached.

---

[1] The Executive Council and Legislative Assembly Ordinance, 1948, Section 18.
[2] *Ibid*, Section 51 (7).

CHAPTER XI

THE REVISION OF THE 1936 TREATY

HAVING presented the dispute in its different phases and analysed its elements, and having shown how the Sudanese emerged as a third party, it is possible to proceed to an examination of the issues raised in the latest phase and to discuss the reasons why no settlement was reached.

The conflict was renewed in 1945 over the revision of the Treaty of Friendship and Alliance signed by Egypt and Great Britain in 1936. The treaty was to be valid for a period of twenty years after which the High Contracting Parties would enter into negotiations for its revision. But a provision was made that such negotiations might be entered upon, with the consent of both parties, any time after the expiration of a period of ten years. The Egyptian Government approached the British Government some months before the expiration of the period of ten years, asking for the revision of the treaty and the British Government readily accepted. Both countries appointed prominent men to their delegations and the negotiations started in 1946 in a cordial atmosphere. But it was unfortunate that at that time the internal political situation in Egypt was even more unsatisfactory than it had been during the negotiations of Sarwat and Mahmoud in 1927 and 1929. Nahas Pasha, who was dismissed by King Farouk in 1944, was out of office. His party refused to contest the general elections held after his dismissal and he refused to join or send Wafdist representatives to the Egyptian delegation. This state of affairs in Egypt contributed to the failure of the negotiations. When Mr. Bevin announced this failure in the House of Commons he expressed his regret that 'in the negotiations His Majesty's Government have had to deal with a minority government'.[1]

The Egyptian delegation demanded the evacuation of Egypt by British troops and the unity of the Sudan with Egypt under the

[1] Papers regarding the negotiations for a revision of the Anglo-Egyptian Treaty of 1936. 1947. Cmd. 7179.

Egyptian Crown. The first demand is not directly connected with the dispute over the Sudan but the evacuation problem has been so closely linked with that of the Sudan in the course of the more recent Anglo-Egyptian attempts to settle the outstanding differences that it demands some brief consideration.

British commercial interests in the Suez Canal and strategic interests in the Middle East have been safeguarded by the stationing of British troops in Egypt and by the provisions of the 1936 Treaty which enabled Britain to have military bases there during the last war.[1] When the Egyptian negotiators demanded in 1946 the evacuation of British troops from their territory the British Foreign Secretary agreed to an evacuation protocol which provided for 'the complete evacuation of Egyptian territory (Egypt) by the British forces . . . by 1st September, 1949'.[2] But the protocol also laid down 'that in the event of Egypt becoming the object of armed aggression or in the event of the United Kingdom becoming involved in war as the result of armed aggression against countries adjacent to Egypt, they shall take, in close co-operation and as a result of consultation, such action as may be recognized as necessary until the Security Council has taken the necessary measures for the re-establishment of peace.'[3] Britain also required that both countries 'undertake not to conclude any alliance and not to take part in any coalition directed against one of them'.[4] The Egyptian Prime Minister agreed to a draft treaty embodying these and other clauses related to them, but, because no agreement was finally reached on the Sudan, Egypt refused to sign the draft treaty initialled by Mr. Bevin and Sidky Pasha.

British strategic interests in Egypt, therefore, became intertwined with the dispute over the Sudan, and they will continue as long as Egypt insists on making the settlement of the two questions interdependent.

With regard to the Sudan, Egypt demanded, in the negotiations for the revision of the treaty of 1936, the termination of the administrative regime established under the 1899 Agreement and

[1] See below p. 68.
[2] Egypt No. 2, 1947, *op. cit.*
[3] *Ibid*, Part I, Annex 1.
[4] *Ibid.*

the recognition of the unity of Egypt and the Sudan under the Egyptian Crown. The only reference made to the type of unity was that it should be a permanent one.

It is clear, however, from the facts given in the preceding four chapters, that any settlement of the Sudan question, if it is not to be effected by force, must be a compromise which would be acceptable to all three parties—the British, the Egyptians and the Sudanese. Mr. Bevin and Sidky Pasha, after the British and Egyptian delegations failed to come to an agreement in Cairo, reached what they considered to be a suitable compromise and annexed it to the draft treaty which they initialled in London in October, 1946. It was called the Draft Sudan Protocol and ran as follows:—

'The Policy which the High Contracting Parties undertake to follow in the Sudan within the framework of the unity between the Sudan and Egypt under the common Crown of Egypt will have for its essential objectives to assure the well-being of the Sudanese, the development of their interests and their active preparation for self-government and consequently the exercise of the right to choose the future status of the Sudan. Until the High Contracting Parties can in full common agreement realize this latter objective after consultation with the Sudanese, the Agreement of 1899 will continue and Article 11 of the Treaty of 1936 . . . will remain in force . . .'[1]

The protocol seems to have attempted to meet all three requirements. In the first place it sought to satisfy Egypt by recognizing a temporary unity between her and the Sudan under the common Crown of Egypt, leaving the question of permanent unity to be decided later. Secondly, it attempted to satisfy the Sudanese by recognizing their rights to self-government and self-determination. Finally it gave Britain the chance to maintain the *status quo*, and, through satisfying Egypt, helped her to secure the agreement of Sidky Pasha to initial the draft treaty of alliance.

No sooner had Sidky Pasha returned to Egypt, however, than reports appeared in the papers that the British Government had agreed to the unity of Egypt and the Sudan permanently under the Egyptian Crown, without giving the Sudanese any right to

[1] *Ibid.* Annex 2.

secede from Egypt.[1] These reports, which were not contradicted by Sidky Pasha, gave rise to a statement in the House of Commons by the Prime Minister on 28th October, 1946 in which he said, '. . . no change in the existing status and administration of the Sudan is contemplated and no impairment of the right of the Sudanese people ultimately to decide their own future.' The reports in the Egyptian press also caused such anxiety in the Sudan, especially among the independence group, that no assurance would convince the Sudanese that Egyptian sovereignty was symbolic and temporary. The writer attended a private meeting of the Advisory Council called by the Governor-General and another meeting of the same body called by the Civil Secretary in which both men laboured in vain to convince the councillors that no change in the *status quo* was contemplated. There was a time when serious disorders were expected in Khartoum and Omdurman where many people were brought in from the provinces by political parties.

These press reports were also followed by official utterances which confirmed Egypt's attitude. Nokrashy Pasha declared in the Chamber of Deputies, 'When I say unity of Egypt and the Sudan under the Egyptian Crown, I mean permanent unity.'[2]

It became clear after such reports and announcements that unless the two parties agreed on an interpretation of the Protocol there was no question of incorporating it in a treaty. When this was attempted Egypt refused to modify her position about self-determination for the Sudanese. The British Government offered Egypt 'the support of the United Kingdom in the maintenance of a Sudan friendly to Egypt, and in particular to safeguard the position of Egypt with regard to the waters of the Nile'.[3] She also proposed the setting up of a joint Anglo-Egyptian-Sudanese machinery to review the progress of the Sudanese towards self-government.[4] None of these proposals was acceptable to Egypt and the British Secretary of State for Foreign Affairs told the House of Commons on 27th January, 1947 that the Egyptian Government

---

[1] A full interpretation was made by Sidky Pasha to the Egyptian weekly *Rose El Yousef* which published it on 20th November, 1946.

[2] Cmd. 7179, 1947, *op. cit.*, p. 6.

[3] *Ibid*,. p. 5.

[4] *Ibid.*

had informed him of their decision to break off negotiations for a revision of the Anglo-Egyptian Treaty of 1936. Thus Egypt refused a draft treaty which would have enabled her to see the evacuation of British troops from her territory by September, 1949, for no reason other than her failure to gain her full demands in the Sudan. It seems incredible that the Egyptians, who have ever since 1882 been agitating for the evacuation of British troops from their territory, and who have always felt that their independence would never be complete so long as those troops were there, should refuse the first promise ever made by Britain to evacuate her troops by a definite appointed date. The only possible explanation may be that the Egyptians, who knew that they had a strong case for demanding the evacuation of British troops, and realized the importance of Anglo-Egyptian alliance to Britain, thought that by making that alliance conditional on meeting their demands in the Sudan they might force the British to accept their terms. The use of the Sudan for political bargaining was mentioned in the Security Council by Nokrashy Pasha and by Sir Alexander Cadogan. Both of them said they would not barter away the future of the Sudanese to gain their political ends.[1]

The step which the Egyptian Government took after they broke off negotiations was to take the whole dispute to the Security Council of the United Nations where it was debated between 5th August and 10th September, 1947. The issues put before the Security Council by Nokrashy Pasha and Sir Alexander Cadogan, who presented the Egyptian and British cases respectively, were the same as those which caused the breaking off of negotiations. The only difference was the way in which Nokrashy Pasha argued against the right of the Sudanese to self-determination. He argued that Egypt and the Sudan had always been one and the same country geographically, ethnically, culturally and politically. He contended that Mohamed Ali's action in 1820 was not a conquest but a 'consolidation of the various parts of Egypt and a unification of its governmental institutions',[2] and that the boundary which existed between the two parts of Egypt was an invention of the

---

[1] S. C. R. 179th Meeting, 11th August, 1947, Section 24, and 182nd Meeting, 13th August, 1947, Section 8.
[2] S. C. R., 175th Meeting, 5th August, 1947, Section 35-38.

British who took the opportunity of their being in Egypt to push their designs on the Sudan.[1]

Having argued in this way he came to the logical conclusion that the question of self-determination did not arise, and insisted that the relations between the two peoples inhabiting the two parts of the Nile Valley were a matter which should be settled by the Egyptians and the Sudanese[2] without any interference from the 'intruding British,' whom he accused of making the question of preparing the Sudanese for self-government and ultimate self-determination an excuse for prolonging their domination of the Sudan in order to serve their own interests. 'I must reiterate the intention of the Egyptian Government', he said, 'to work in season and out of season to protect the Sudan from dismemberment, to make it possible for our Sudanese brethren to direct their own affairs within the framework of the unity of the Nile Valley under the Crown of Egypt.'[3] He further argued that the British, who were alien to the Sudanese in every respect, were not qualified to guide the social and cultural development of the Sudan and to prepare the Sudanese for self-government.

For these reasons he asked the Security Council to determine the administrative regime which had been maintained by the British since 1899, so that the Sudanese might share the welfare and aspiration of their fellow countrymen in Egypt.[4]

The line which was taken by Nokrashy Pasha, has in recent years also been taken by Egyptian politicians and writers. Dr. Mohammed Shafik Ghorbal and other eminent Egyptian scholars, to quote a few instances, contribute the same views about the unity of Egypt and the Sudan in an official Egyptian publication,[5] and Abdel Rahman El Rafi follows the same theme in his 'History of the National Movement.'[6]

It will be noticed from the facts given in the previous chapters—particularly Chapter IV—that Nokrashy Pasha chose a poor basis for his argument. This is, however, understandable because he

[1] Ibid.
[2] Ibid., Section 15 and 43.
[3] S. C. R., 193rd Meeting, 22nd August, 1947, Section 9.
[4] S. C. R., 175th Meeting, 5th August, 1947, Section 19.
[5] Shafik Ghorbal, op. cit., especially p. 61.
[6] History of the National Movement (about 12 volumes); see especially Vol. III. (The Era of Mohammed Ali, Cairo, 1947, p. 128).

could not have based his claim of permanent unity on the right of conquest which is, to say the least, repugnant to the spirit of the United Nations Charter. Nokrashy Pasha heard the representative of Poland say, after accepting the validity of the 1899 Agreement, 'As I have already stated, although the right of conquest was a title recognized by international law at a time when the Treaty with the Khedive of Egypt was concluded, by no means can it be applied to-day when the Charter of the United Nations excludes that right as a title at any time and at any place.'[1] Nokrashy Pasha could have put the emphasis on Egypt's vital interests in the Sudan, but the course of the discussion showed that he would never have succeeded in persuading the Security Council to accept those interests as a basis for his claim for permanent unity.

Sir Alexander Cadogan used the same arguments as those adopted by Mr. Bevin during the abortive negotiations.

No sooner had the Security Council started to discuss the case than it became clear that its members unanimously upheld the right of the Sudanese to determine the future status of their country. 'The Polish Government', said the representative of Poland, 'has always been animated, in the solution of national problems, by the spirit of the self-determination of nations and peoples, and we believe that this principle should be applied to the case under discussion.'[2]

Mr. Gromyko, speaking for the U.S.S.R., said, 'We do not know what the wishes of the Sudanese people are nor what are their aspirations. Without the precise knowledge of the aspirations of the Sudanese people, it is difficult for the Security Council to make any decision on this question.'[3] A third example is the opinion of the Chinese representative. 'The Sudanese people', he said, 'should have the fullest and freest right of self-determination, which is the foundation of the Charter of the United Nations . . .'[4]

[1] S. C. R., 182nd Meeting, 13th August, 1947, Section 28.
[2] Ibid., Section 33.
[3] S. C. R., 189th Meeting, 20th August, 1947, Section 16.
[4] Ibid., Section 19. For Similar evidence see the views of the Representatives of Australia, France and Colombia, S. C. R. 196th Meeting, 26th August, 1947, Sections 25 and 26, 198th Meeting, 28th August, 1947, Sections 14 and 40 respectively. The representatives of U.S.A., Brazil and Syria voted in favour of the Colombian resolution which gave the Sudanese the right of self-determination, S. C. R., 200th Meeting, 29th August, 1947, Section 33.

Nokrashy Pasha, seeing that his position had become untenable after the members of the Security Council expressed their views, agreed that the Sudanese were entitled to self-determination, but objected to such right being exercised under British rule or with British aid. 'I am confident,' he told the Council, 'that when the Sudanese are free to express themselves they and the Egyptians will reach mutually satisfactory solutions which will accord with the democratic principles of the Charter.'[1]

The right of the Sudanese to determine their future, therefore, received not only the support of the United Kingdom, but that of the Security Council and even that of the Prime Minister of Egypt, and must therefore be regarded as recognized by the whole world. The only difficulty which remains is the recognition of this fact by those who succeeded Nokrashy Pasha, for, in Egypt, as elsewhere what is accepted by one Prime Minister is not always regarded as binding on his successors. Nahas Pasha, who is at the time of writing (1950) Prime Minister of Egypt, cabled to the Secretary General of the United Nations, when he was out of office, informing him that Nokrashy Pasha was not a true representative of the Egyptian people.

The Security Council, having failed to adopt any resolution on the method by which the disputants should settle their differences, shelved the whole question. Britain and Egypt did not approach each other for further negotiations for the settlement of all outstanding issues until late in 1950, but negotiations were entered upon for the settlement of the methods of training the Sudanese for self-government. These were conducted in Cairo in May, 1948 by the British Ambassador and the Egyptian Foreign Minister. They came to an agreement but it was rejected by the Foreign Relations Committee of the Egyptian Senate.[2] At this point the British Government gave the Governor-General of the Sudan unilateral authorization to proceed with his proposals for taking the Sudanese a step further on the road to self-government. He promulgated the Executive Council and Legislative Assembly Ordinance in June, 1948 and formally opened the Assembly in December of the

[1] S. C. R., 196th Meeting, 26th August, 1947, Section 29.
[2] An *official communiqué* was issued to the press in Khartoum in June, 1948 giving the points on which agreement was reached.

same year. He incorporated in the Ordinance the recommendations of the British Ambassador and the Egyptian Foreign Minister which were rejected by the Senate Committee.

The first day of September, 1949, the date by which Mr. Bevin had agreed to evacuate all British troops from Egypt, came and went and the relations between Egypt and Britain were no better than they had been when the case was taken to the Security Council. Not only was there no improvement in Anglo-Egyptian relations but new developments made it more difficult for Egypt to get Britain's agreement to her demands of evacuation and the unity of the Nile Valley. The intensification of the 'cold war', the coming of Israel and the armed intervention in Korea, have created for Britain as well as for Egypt new problems in the defence of the Middle East. The progress of the Sudanese towards self-government through the Legislative Assembly and the Executive Council, and their insistence on being treated in the same way as the comparatively less advanced former Italian Colonies of Libya and Somaliland were treated by the United Nations, made the chances of a permanent unity of the Nile Valley under the Egyptian Crown more remote.

It was not until the summer of 1950 that exploratory talks started between the British Ambassador and the Egyptian Government in Cairo to find a basis for renewed negotiations on a revision of the 1936 Treaty. These were preceded by talks by military experts on matters relating to the defence of the Middle East. The talks were progressing quietly and in a 'cordial atmosphere'[1] until King Farouk, in his Speech from the Throne on 16th November, 1950, which was read by Nahas Pasha, the Prime Minister, said: 'My Government considers that the 1936 Treaty has lost its validity as a basis for Anglo-Egyptian relations, and it deems it inevitable that it should be abrogated.' Egyptian members of Parliament were also told that it was necessary that future relations should be founded upon new principles which they should approve, namely the immediate and complete evacuation and the unification of the Nile Valley under the Egyptian Crown.

---

[1] *Communiqués* issued by the Foreign Office on 2nd and 8th September, 1950. *The Times*, 4th and 9th September, 1950.

This intention of proclaiming unilaterally the abrogation both of the 1936 Treaty and of the Agreement of 1899 angered the British people and members of Parliament. It was answered by Mr. Bevin in a statement to the House of Commons on 20th November, 1950. He pointed out that the treaty of 1936, which was ratified by the parliaments of both countries, cannot be modified except by mutual consent. On the question of the evacuation of British troops, which have since the failure of the 1946 negotiations been evacuated from Cairo by Britain of her own accord and concentrated in the Canal Zone, Mr. Bevin's attitude was quite different from that adopted with Sidky Pasha when he initialled the evacuation protocol in 1946. 'The Egyptian Government', he said, 'have stated that they wish all British forces to be withdrawn from the Canal Zone in time of peace. The principle of common defence measures in time of peace has been accepted by all the western Powers and is fully compatible with national independence and sovereignty. Other countries in the Middle East are co-operating in this way.

'This is not a matter which merely concerns the United Kingdom and Egypt. What is at stake is the safety and independence of other countries also. I can assure them, as I assure the House, that His Majesty's Government have no intention of taking any steps or agreeing to any measures which would leave the Middle East defenceless, or would needlessly prejudice the safety of free and friendly countries in that area and elsewhere.'

With regard to the Sudan he reiterated his previous statement.[1] 'That country', he said in the same statement, 'has been the scene of great progress in the political social and economic field during recent years. It would be tragic if anything were to disturb this. His Majesty's Government's attitude remains the same. It is briefly that the Sudanese should in due course freely decide their own future.'

In spite of these difficulties Mr. Bevin told the House of Commons that he did not despair of being able to reconcile differences with Egypt on a friendly and just basis. He invited the Egyptian Foreign Minister for talks in London but, up to the time of writing (December, 1950) no agreement was reached. It seems unlikely

[1] See above p. 112.

that any agreement can be reached unless Egypt is prepared to agree to a compromise. The official utterances of her spokesmen do not indicate any change in the attitude adopted in the Security Council and in the Speech from the Throne on 16th November, 1950.[1]

[1] For further developments see chapter XIV.

PART FOUR

THE EFFECTS
ON THE SUDAN

CHAPTER XII

THE POLITICAL EFFECTS

SUDANESE society, with very few exceptions, is not charac-
terized by any marked economic inequality which produces
a class system. The divisions which exist to-day originated
from either religion, tribalism or the new educational system.
Before the rise of the Mahdi, individual members of Sudanese
tribes in the north enjoyed that equality of status which is characteristic of nomad Arab society. Members of the negroid tribes of
the south enjoyed within their social structure the same equality
of status. The loyalty of the individual in both parts of the country
was to his tribe rather than to any bigger unit.

When the Mahdi came, he unified the tribes of the north in a
way similar to that in which the Prophet welded together the
tribes of the Arabian Peninsula. But those religious leaders who
did not accept the Mahdi's mission remained outside this union.
When the Mahdi's regime was destroyed in 1899, religious persecution came to an end, and there appeared two main religious
sects. The first is the 'Ansar', or supporters of the Mahdi who are
now under the leadership of Sir Sayid Abdel Rahman El Mahdi,
the virtual leader, as we have seen, of the Umma party which
stands for independence. There is a prevalent allegation that
the Mahdi aspires to be king of an independent Sudan. The
second sect is the 'Khatmia', the followers of the orthodox leader,
Sayid Mohammed Osman El Mirghani, which is now led by Sir
Sayid Ali El Mirghani, whose main object is to oppose any
independence movement which aims at crowning the son of the
Mahdi.

Tribalism, which was dealt a serious blow by the Mahdi,
emerged in the early days of the present era as a weak social
institution, but was later revived when the system of 'native administration' came to be established after 1920. Tribal chiefs, who

were built up by the Government, gradually gained prestige and political power.[1] They are a force in the first Legislative Assembly[2] which directs the internal policy and which may one day decide the destiny of the country.

The new educational system is producing what may be called an educated *élite* following to a great extent the political and social ideals of the West. They are slowly but surely taking over the leadership of the country in social, political and economic affairs.

This brief sketch and the account given in Chapter X show the incoherence of political life at this stage of Sudanese progress towards full nationhood. They also show how much wider a political controversy can be made when conflicting external pressures, such as the persuasion which may be brought to bear by the disputing Co-domini, are added to the already existing internal divisions. The Sudanese have been faced with the temptation of attempting certain tactics in order to influence these external forces.

This lack of solidarity among the Sudanese cannot be attributed solely to the fact that the Sudan has been under the tutelage of constantly disputing Co-domini. One might even say that the dispute is not responsible for creating the ingredients of disunity among the Sudanese. What can be said is that the dispute precipitated and fostered disunion amongst the educated elements. It is also to some extent responsible for the cleavage between two sects of the same religion since these failed to reach a compromise on political matters such as that reached by the members of two different religious communities in Egypt—the Moslems and the Copts.

There is ample evidence that in the two periods of intensive political activity which followed the two world wars the educated Sudanese began with one common aim, that of the independence of the Sudan. Later, in each period they split into two camps, one seeking independence and the other a form of unity with Egypt. There were two reasons for this. The first was that those who sought unity with Egypt in both periods did so after they thought

[1] Fabian Society, *The Sudan, the Road Ahead*, London, 1945, p. 12.
[2] Over half the 85 Sudanese members of the Assembly are tribal chiefs: see official list of the members of the Executive Council and Legislative Assembly, Khartoum, 1949.

that the Sudan Government, which to them represented the British Government alone and not the Governments of both Britain and Egypt, was not sympathetic with Sudanese aspirations for independence. The second was that Egypt did her best by various means to win the educated Sudanese to her side.

Ali Abdel Latif, who became in 1924 the leader of the 'White Flag League', was in 1921 the active organizing member of the 'Sudanese United Tribes Society'[1] which was working for an independent Sudan. He, as head of the latter society, published a document in 1922 which proves his earlier stand for independence. The document contained the following two clauses:—

'7. As God created us free we object to be the slaves of any nation, but as the country still requires instruction, the nation has the right to choose what power to rule: on conditions and for a fixed period.

'9. We do not wish to be governed by a foreign ruler and the nation should select as their ruler one of the *Ashraf* (religious Sudanese men descending from the Prophet), the remaining *Ashraf* to be as ministers, and so forth the chiefs of tribes.'[2]

Ali Abdel Latif was prosecuted and sent to prison for publishing this document, which was considered 'exciting disaffection' to the Sudan Government. This he regarded as lack of sympathy with Sudanese aspirations on the part of the Sudan Government. From that date onwards he became an ardent supporter of the unity of the Nile Valley under the Egyptian Crown, and for this object he set up his second society, that of the White Flag League. The writer was informed by several of Abdel Latif's colleagues that the sole object behind the White Flag League was to impress upon the British that, unless they would agree to the independence of the Sudan, the Sudanese would have no alternative but to join hands with Egypt. This is exactly what happened in Congress in 1942. Then the less moderate members of that organization, those who formed the Ashigga party, made the 'Unity of the Nile Valley' under the Egyptian Crown their goal, following the refusal by the Sudan Government of the memorandum which had been put

[1] Information obtained from a note prepared for the writer by the Civil Secretary's Department, Khartoum, on political societies, 1920-1924.

[2] From an English translation of the document provided by the Civil Secretary's Office, Khartoum.

forward by a Congress united in its pursuit of independence.[1] It is
true that the swing over in both cases was largely due to those
politicians attributing lack of sympathy to the Sudan Government
which, because it had a British head and British nationals in all
the responsible posts, was considered to all intents and purposes
to represent the views of the British Government alone. But it is
also equally true that Egyptian propaganda and funds were in
both periods responsible for winning sections of the Sudanese over
to the Egyptian side to strengthen Egypt's case for sovereignty
over the Sudan and for its control. The influence of Egyptian
propaganda in the first period is fully described in the works of
men who held posts in Egypt and the Sudan,[2] and is mentioned
in the writings of independent men.[3] Its influence in the second
period has even been greater. This was exerted through the Egyptian press which was widely read in the Sudan; through the
Egyptian officers of the two battalions of the Egyptian Army
stationed in the Sudan; through the officials of the Egyptian Irrigation Service and of the Department of the Economic Expert in
Khartoum; and through missions of various kinds which Egypt
sent to the Sudan. Egyptian funds were also liberally expended to
assist Sudanese delegations to Cairo, London and America, and to
help the families of Sudanese politicians on the unity side who were
imprisoned for inciting hatred against the present regime in the
Sudan.[4]

The British have also been accused in both periods of using
their position as virtual rulers of the country to exclude the
Egyptians and Egyptian influence in the Sudan and to encourage
separatist movements in the country.[5] The British people and the
British Government, as opposed to the Egyptian people and the
Egyptian Government, cannot be accused of employing the sort of
propaganda which Egypt used. No British private or public
funds were spent in the Sudan for furthering any cause. The
geographical situation of Britain does not allow of close contacts,
and the British press which reaches the Sudan is limited in volume

---

[1] Chapter x above.
[2] Lloyd, Vol. II, pp. 133-34; MacMichael, p. 149.
[3] Pierre Crabitès, *The Winning of the Sudan*, London, 1934, p. 185.
[4] *Al Misri*, Wafdist daily paper published in Cairo, 1st January, 1949.
[5] Nokrashy Pasha, S. C. R. 175th Meeting, 5th August, 1947, Section 43.

and is read by a very small number of educated Sudanese. But any one who lived in the Sudan could not fail to notice that the sentiments of the British officials in the Sudan Government were with the independence groups. The influence of these officials, especially that of the District Commissioner who has direct contact with the inhabitants and chiefs of his district, has, no doubt, been strong. These sentiments were implicit in a secret directive circulated by the Civil Secretary of the Sudan Government to all senior British officials.[1]

Another effect of the dispute is that it tempted Sudanese politicians to toy with the idea of playing off the disputing Co-domini against each other in order to extract from them the widest possible concessions. One of the aims of the Sudanese delegation which was sent to Cairo by the unity parties was to deter Egypt from separating the question of the Sudan from her other outstanding questions in the 1946 negotiations. They believed that once Egypt succeeded in evacuating British troops from her territory she would not stand firm on the question of terminating the existing regime in the Sudan. Here again the Sudanese were divided and differences of opinion between them over this question widened the gap created by the activities of the co-domini. These temptations into which the Sudanese were led have no parallel in other dependent territories where there is generally a straight issue between the imperial ruler and the colonial subjects.

A further effect of the dispute was that it made the future status of the Sudan overshadow all political issues, disagreement over which is normally the reason for the formation of parties. A glance through the programmes of Sudanese parties is enough to prove this. The Sudanese press and political talk in public and private places was dominated by the future status of the Sudan.

Another serious effect is the lack of trust between the Sudanese and the Co-domini and between the Sudanese themselves. When the Sudanese read the charges made practically every day by the

---

[1] Secret document No. SCR/36.M.8 of 9th April, 1945, stolen for the Egyptian paper *Al Balagh* and published on 18th March, 1947. The Public Relations Officer of the Sudan Government told *Sawt El Sudan,* that the translation and contents of the document were correct. *Sawt El Sudan,* 31st March, 1947. The writer, as a senior official in the Sudan Government, had access to some of these circulars before he relinquished his post in December, 1946.

Egyptian press and wireless against British policy and actions in the Sudan, and when they consider the charges and counter-charges, such as the ones made by Nokrashy Pasha and Sir Alexander Cadogan in the Security Council, many of them, especially the younger enthusiastic ones, could hardly be expected to have faith in the intentions professed either by Britain or by Egypt to lead the Sudan on the road to self-government and ultimate independence.

This lack of confidence also prevailed strongly between the rival independence and unity parties. Both fronts have staged demonstrations at intervals since the opening of the latest phase of the dispute. Although the official aim of the demonstrations was to support the political claims of the rival fronts, they were also staged to show the superiority in numbers over the opposite party. The Independence Front, to quote one instance, held a demonstration on 30th October, 1946, and the National Front held a counter demonstration on 1st November. The writer saw these demonstrations and he could not help feeling that this other purpose was at least as important as the more publicized political aims. There was a time when their respective papers, owned by the two rival religious leaders, poured abuse at each other and called the leaders of the opposite party traitors.[1] Such newspaper warfare, especially when the two religious leaders were the subject of criticism, very nearly led to outbreaks of serious disorder.

In the case of the two chief religious leaders, the dispute had no effect during the period of intense political activity which followed the first world war. They were united in their pursuit of an independent Sudan. When Lord Allenby visited Khartoum in April, 1922, he received a deputation of 40 notables, headed by Sir Sayid Ali El Mirghani. They 'expressed their views that the Sudan was a distinct country and nationality and should be allowed to progress on its own lines of development'.[2] But the two religious leaders were no longer united during the latest phase. Sir Sayid Abdel Rahman El Mahdi relied on the British Government's reluctance to put the Sudan under Egyptian sovereignty,

---

[1] *El Umma* (Mahdist) and *Sawt El Sudan* (Mirghanist) August—December, 1947.

[2] From a note prepared for the writer by the Civil Secretary's Department, Khartoum.

while Sir Sayid Ali El Mirghani, interpreting British support for the Sudanese right of self-determination to mean support for his opponent, leaned on the Egyptian side.

These instances illustrate the disintegrating effects of the dispute on Sudanese political life. They show beyond doubt the inherent disadvantages of condominium rule. There seems to be little doubt that if the dispute continues it will do irreparable damage to Sudanese unity. The writer more than once heard it suggested that the dispute had its advantages in that it hastened political awakening and constitutional development and also kept the British 'on their toes'. There may be some truth in this. But even if it was altogether true the disadvantages mentioned here and in the next chapter heavily outweigh the advantages.

CHAPTER XIII

THE CONSTITUTIONAL EFFECTS

A DESCRIPTION of the 1899 Agreement, which served as the constitutional charter of the Sudan for the last fifty years, was given in Chapter IV. Reference was also made in Chapter X to the steps taken in 1944 and 1948 to associate the Sudanese more closely with the government of their country. It was stated that the British and Egyptian Governments, while agreeing in principle upon training the Sudanese for self-government, disagreed over the manner in which they should be trained.[1] It remains here to show the reasons for their disagreement and to show in what way constitutional development was affected by the dispute.

The Governor-General of the Sudan submitted on 22nd August, 1947, proposals to the British and Egyptian Governments for the setting up of an Executive Council and a Legislative Assembly in the Sudan, and asked them to consider them in principle. The British Ambassador in Cairo, in reply, informed the Governor-General that 'His Majesty's Government have no comments to offer on these proposals which are, they consider, well calculated to achieve the proclaimed purposes of the Co-domini, namely the progressive development of self-government in the Sudan.'[2]

The reply of the Egyptian Prime Minister accepted the proposals in principle but disagreed with the Governor-General about the details and suggested certain modifications.

The Prime Minister wrote:—'Since the Royal Egyptian Government are sincerely desirous—as emphasised on several occasions—to enable the Sudanese to govern themselves and are not willing that the Sudanese should lose any opportunity of having the maximum share of responsibility of government accorded to them, the Royal Egyptian Government, notwithstanding that the Anglo-Egyptian dispute is still pending, deem it their duty—while

[1] See above p. 113.
[2] *No. 207* dated Cairo, 23rd October, 1947.
463/34/47.

fully maintaining their position which had been clearly defined before the Security Council—to accept participation, for the time being, in drawing up a regime which would pave the way to self-government, provided this regime be free from the defects pointed out in the attached note and provided that it fulfils the requirements outlined in the said note. Thus the delay in settling the Anglo-Egyptian dispute will not retard the progress of the Sudanese, for any period, on the road to self-government.'[1]

The criticisms were directed towards the narrow franchise,[2] the limited powers of the legislative assembly in not having the final word in passing the budget and approving the legislation, and the fact that there was no reference to Egyptian participation with the British in training the Sudanese for self-government.

Further correspondence followed between the Governor-General and the Egyptian Prime Minister but no agreement was reached. Finally the British and Egyptian Governments agreed that the British Ambassador in Cairo and the Egyptian Minister for Foreign Affairs should meet and discuss the differences. 'With the agreement of the Governor-General they suggested that a tripartite Anglo-Egyptian-Sudanese Committee should be set up to supervise the progress of the Sudanese towards self-government, and that an Anglo-Egyptian Committee should supervise the elections to the Legislative Assembly.'[3] In addition to this the Governor-General expressed his willingness to nominate to the Executive Council two Egyptians from among the Egyptian officials serving in the Sudan, and also agreed that the Senior Staff Officer of the Egyptian forces in the Sudan should attend all meetings of the Executive Council when defence matters were being discussed.'[4] The agreement reached was, however, rejected by the Foreign Relations Committee of the Egyptian Senate because it gave Egypt an insufficient number of seats on the Executive Council, and because it did not provide for giving the two Egyptians on the Executive Council ministerial posts in the future administration. This led to a complete deadlock and the British

[1] No. 92-3/37 dated Cairo 26th November, 1947.
[2] See above p. 113.
[3] From a statement by the Under Secretary of State for Foreign Affairs made in the House of Commons on 14th June, 1948. 5th Series, Vol. 452, col. 20.
[4] *Ibid.*

Government decided to take unilateral action. The Under Secretary of State for Foreign Affairs made a Statement in the House of Commons on 14th June, 1948 in which he said, 'His Majesty's Government therefore feel that they can no longer stand in the way of the Governor-General doing as he thinks fit regarding the promulgation of the Ordinance (creating the Executive Council and the Legislative Assembly) in accordance with his duties and obligations for the government of the Sudan under the Agreement of 1899.'[1] On the next day the Governor-General promulgated the ordinance.

As the Governor-General retained the power to veto the decisions of the Executive Council and the Legislative Assembly,[2] and as the Ordinance laid down that bills passed by the Assembly and the Executive Council shall not become law until he has given his assent and proclaimed them as law, his promulgation of the Ordinance without the prior consent of Egypt can hardly be regarded as a violation of the 1899 Agreement which holds him solely responsible for the government of the Sudan.

It is clear from this that the dispute had a delaying effect on Sudanese constitutional progress. The proposals which were submitted by the Governor-General to the Co-domini in August, 1947 were not put into effect until the end of 1948. A delay of a year or two may not be a long one but it must be remembered that if the Governor-General had not acted upon the unilateral approval of the stronger partner in the Condominium, constitutional progress might have had to wait for an indefinite time.

Secondly, as the Egyptian Government and the Egyptian press regarded the new institutions as puppets designed to serve British and pro-British interests in the Sudan, Egyptian opposition encouraged the 'Unity of the Nile Valley' parties to boycott the Assembly. It would be unfair to the Sudanese who boycotted the election in 1948 to say that they did so solely because of Egyptian pressure or persuasion. Sir Sayid Ali El Mirghani and his supporters and the Unionist party have declared on several occasions that if certain reforms were introduced in the electoral law and

---

[1] *Ibid.*

[2] The Governor-General's veto of the Legislative Assembly's decisions on bills can, however, only be exercised after reference to the British and Egyptian Governments.

in the powers of the Assembly they would contest the elections. Nevertheless, the withholding of Egyptian approval made the Ashigga Party declare that its members would not accept the Assembly 'even if it was free from all defects' so long as it was formed under the existing regime in the Sudan.

Thirdly, the dispute deprived the Sudan of the existence of a body to supervise the planned progress of the Sudan towards self-government. The British Government proposed the setting up of a 'Joint Council which will meet as often as is necessary to keep under review the progress of the Sudanese towards self-government, to make appropriate reports to the two Governments, and to recommend in due course suitable arrangements for ascertaining what are the wishes of the Sudanese people and for giving effect thereto.'[1] It was also proposed that the Sudanese should be represented on this council. The proposal was rejected by Egypt twice, once in 1946 during the negotiations and again in 1948 when the British Ambassador and the Egyptian Minister for Foreign Affairs met in Cairo. The result is a continuous tension between the Governor-General and the Sudanese who aspire for further development. Had there been such a council the Governor-General would have been in a much more favourable position to secure the co-operation of all the Sudanese. Now he is in the awkward position of being, as the Arabs say, the judge and the adversary in the case.

Finally, and this is by far the most serious effect, as the Governor-General cannot exceed the powers conferred on him by the 1899 Agreement, he cannot, under present arrangements, give the Sudanese full self-government since he has to retain his power of veto. So even self-government, on which Egypt and Britain are agreed, cannot be given to the Sudanese unless Britain and Egypt agree to amend or cancel the 1899 Agreement. The result will either be a retardation of Sudanese constitutional progress and frustration of the people, or political trouble in the country.

The dispute, however, had some advantages. The criticisms made by the Egyptian Government in their note addressed to the Governor-General and the British Government on 26th November, 1947 helped to improve the Ordinance creating the Council

[1] Cmd. 7179, 1947, *op. cit.*

and the Assembly in a number of ways. They made the Sudan Government consider with greater care the electoral rules; they helped to increase the powers of the Assembly; and they were to some measure responsible for the appointment of responsible Sudanese Ministers. Nevertheless, the disadvantages of the dispute as stated previously were, in the view of the writer, much greater than the advantages.

FUTURE PROSPECTS

CHAPTER XIV

FUTURE PROSPECTS

AN attempt has been made in this book to analyse the Egyptian dispute over the Sudan in the different phases through which it passed since it began in 1883. It is very clear from this long story that it is extremely difficult if, indeed, not impossible, for a student of history to predict the kind of settlement which will be acceptable by all parties and how and when it can be reached. Two things seem, however, to be almost certain: the first is that Great Britain and Egypt will not agree on a settlement and, even if they agree on one, it seems almost certain that they will disagree on how and when it should be effected. This is because the main difficulty in reaching a settlement, which lies behind all of this prolonged dispute, has been the great difference in power and in character between the disputants. We have, on the one hand, a powerful country, at some stages of the dispute the strongest imperialist power in the world, determined to safeguard her interests, and which, nevertheless, because of her long experience in diplomacy, was skilled in the art of compromise and used that skill in the gradual settlement of her disputes with other nations. On the other hand, we have a weak country which was swept over by successive waves of strong, twentieth century nationalism which scarcely leave a nation in a mood to accept fractional terms. 'Either full independence or quick death' was the slogan given to the Egyptian people by their greatest nationalist leader, Zaghlul Pasha, after the first world war.

Agreement between Britain and Egypt about the Sudan is even more difficult to attain because of the association of the Sudan dispute in the minds of the Egyptian people and statesmen with the question of the evacuation of British forces from Egyptian soil. This has been, and may continue to be, a stumbling block in the way of a settlement which will satisfy all parties concerned especially in these days when the Western Powers regard the defence of the Suez Canal and the Middle East so vital to the safety of their interests.

The reader can scarcely have failed to come to the conclusion that it does seem almost certain that Britain and Egypt will not agree on a settlement by such methods as seeking a solution by negotiation, enquiry, mediation, conciliation, arbitration, judicial settlement, or any other kind of peaceful means within the disputants' choice—methods suggested in Article 33 of the United Nations Charter. Great Britain and Egypt tried many kinds of negotiations between 1920 and 1951, eight of which were formal, without reaching a final settlement. At the end of the last formal negotiations Egypt abrogated the 1936 Treaty and the 1899 Agreements by unilateral action. Britain refused to recognize this and the two countries reached the worst deadlock in the history of the dispute. Egypt also took the dispute to the Security Council in 1947 but the general opinion expressed by the Council produced no results. We find that the disputants, after they left the Security Council, disagreed over the methods to be adopted in training the Sudanese for self-government; and, if it were not for the unilateral action taken by Britain to establish the Legislative Assembly and reconstitute the Executive Council, the progress of the Sudanese towards self-government would have been retarded if not completely stopped.

Seeking a solution by other methods such as appointing a fact finding commission or a conciliation commission for conducting an enquiry and making proposals, or appointing arbitrators or taking the dispute to the International Court of Justice, does not seem to have better prospects than bilateral negotiations or taking the dispute to the Security Council. Even in the unlikely chance of the two parties coming to terms, there is no guarantee that any proposal or decision which may be made will be enforced unless it was acceptable to both parties, a contingency which does not seem to be probable.

The second thing that seems to be almost certain is that the continuance of any delay in reaching a settlement must be very harmful to the Sudanese. Their progress towards full self-government and self-determination will either be retarded or, if sponsored by Britain alone, will proceed in an atmosphere which will widen the chasm between those who believe in independence and those who believe in a form of unity with Egypt. The ill effects of Anglo-Egyptian disagreement on Sudanese political and constitutional development were mentioned earlier in Chapters XII and XIII.

Let us now examine possible settlements for the dispute and discuss the ways in which they could be effected.

One of the settlements is the immediate unity of the Nile Valley, that is Egypt and the Sudan, under the Egyptian Crown. This is the settlement which Egypt has always wanted. It is also one which some sections of Sudanese opinion have advocated either out of conviction or as political tactics which they considered would enable them to get rid of the British sooner than they could otherwise do. When the Egyptian Government abrogated the 1936 Treaty and the 1899 Agreements in October, 1951, they approved legislation giving King Farouk the title of King of Egypt and the Sudan and providing for a form of local autonomy for the Sudan. By the provisions of the 'Sudan Decree' the Sudan is to have its own Constituent Assembly, its own electoral law, a separate Council of Ministers and one or two Legislative Chambers. The King of Egypt is given the right to dismiss Sudanese Ministers and to dissolve the Sudanese parliament. Matters concerning foreign affairs, the army, defence and currency, are vested in the hands of the King. He also has the power of giving or refusing his approval to legislation passed by the Sudanese parliament.

A settlement like this can only be justified if all or the majority of the Sudanese indicate that they wish it. It is very difficult to assess the wishes of the people of the Sudan before a plebiscite is held. But it is well known that the Umma party, small independence groups like the Republican party, the vast majority of tribal leaders, and a considerable number of unorganized, educated individuals do not wish to be united with Egypt under the Egyptian Crown. Indeed, not even all the Sudanese parties which desire a form of unity with Egypt give their support to the form of unity which Egypt officially declared. The National Front and the Unionist party, though agreeable to uniting the Sudan with Egypt under the Egyptian Crown, have never desired a permanent unity and have always advocated wider autonomy for the

Sudan. It is, therefore, evident that the Egyptian conception of the Unity of the Nile Valley cannot have any validity unless it could get the support of the majority of the Sudanese in a free plebiscite. The Egyptian action is repugnant to the accepted principles of the United Nations Charter and is for this reason unacceptable as a settlement.

Even if the settlement which Egypt decided to impose on the Sudanese and on her partner in the Condominium had strong legal support it must be ruled out as a solution of the dispute for the simple reason that it is not in Egypt's power to bring to an end the present administration of the Sudan and substitute her own system. This Chapter was revised two months after the signing of the 'Sudan Decree' and the writer could not observe or foresee any indications of the termination of the Condominium regime as a result of the Egyptian action.

Have the Sudanese themselves got a settlement, and could they enforce it? The Sudanese, as mentioned earlier in the chapter on the Emergence of the Sudanese, have not all the same objectives. Some want to be independent, others want to have a relation with Egypt similar to that of the British dominions with the United Kingdom, and there is a small group which wants complete amalgamation with Egypt. But none of these groups can as yet force its will upon the Condominium powers. The political pressure which they could bring to bear has been limited to street demonstrations, protests, some rioting during which a few people were killed, and the boycotting of the Advisory Council and the Legislative Assembly by those who did not accept the policy of gradual advance towards self-government which has been followed by the British Government. None of these, of course, is enough to produce sufficient pressure upon Great Britain and Egypt to induce them to accept Sudanese terms, especially since the Sudanese are not united. The strong weapon used against the Sudan Government as an employer of labour was that of strikes by the workers of the Sudan Railways, and by other trade unions. In these strikes, which date back to 1947, the trade unions have shown a high degree of organization and discipline. A railway strike lasted for over a month in 1947 and there were several strikes of shorter duration. The professed aim of these strikes has been to gain for the working man better wages and better conditions of work and living. Trade Union leaders have on several occasions declared that they did not intend to participate in politics but the day when the labour movement will begin to play an important part in the political affairs of the country is not likely to be long delayed. When that day comes the weapon of strikes and disobedience may be much more effective than the methods so far adopted by the political parties. A *quick* settlement of the dispute by the Sudanese themselves must, therefore, be ruled out as a likely possibility.

The settlement decided upon by the British Government was to train the Sudanese gradually for self-government and to leave it to them to choose their own status as and when they reach that stage. This decision dates back to 3rd November, 1945, when they authorized the Governor-General to assure the Advisory Council for the Northern Sudan of 'the Government's firm intention to consult the people of the Sudan regarding the future of their country'.[1] This was reiterated to the same council on 26th March, 1946 in a statement by the Governor-General in which he informed the members that the object of the Sudan Government was to establish organs of self-government and that 'His Majesty's Government look forward to the day when the Sudanese will be able finally to decide their political future for themselves'.[2]

This policy is in keeping with Article 1[3] of the United Nations Charter which states that one of the purposes of the United Nations is to develop self-determination of peoples. It is also in accordance with Article 73 which states in section (b) that one of the recognized principles is 'to develop self-government, to take due account of the political aspirations of the peoples, and to assist them in the progressive development of their free political institutions . . . '

This British policy, as shown in Chapter XI, was endorsed by the Security Council in 1947, and the Governor-General, supported by the British Government, established the

---

[1] *Proceedings of the Advisory Council for the Northern Sudan, 4th Session, 3rd November* 1945.
[2] *Ibid.*, 5th Session, 17th April, 1946.

Legislative Assembly and the Executive Council in 1948 and has taken measures in 1951 to give the Sudanese 'a self-governing constitution which will satisfy the immediate aspirations of the Sudanese people before the end of 1952'.[1] The Governor-General's policy was supported by the British Labour Government before they were defeated in the general election and by the Conservative Government in a statement made to the House of Commons by Mr. Eden on 15th November, 1951, in which he said, 'His Majesty's Government are glad to note that the Sudan has for some time been, and is now, moving rapidly in the direction of self-government. In their view this progress can, and should, continue on the lines already laid down. His Majesty's Government will, therefore, give the Governor-General their full support for the steps he is taking to bring the Sudanese rapidly to the stage of self-government as a prelude to self-determination . . . His Majesty's Government are glad to know that a constitution providing for self-government may be completed and in operation by the end of 1952.

Having attained self-government, it will be for the Sudanese people to choose their own future status and relationship with the United Kingdom and with Egypt: His Majesty's Government consider that the attainment of self-government should immediately be followed by active preparations for the ultimate goal of self-determination. They will fully support the Governor-General in his effort to ensure that the Sudanese people shall be able to exercise their choice in complete freedom and in full consciousness of their responsibility.'[2]

The British Government tried to gain Egypt's co-operation in the fulfilment of this policy on three occasions. It will be recalled that they offered Sidky Pasha 'the support of the United Kingdom in the maintenance of a Sudan friendly to Egypt, and in particular to safeguard the position of Egypt with regard to the waters of the Nile'. They also proposed the setting up of a joint Anglo-Egyptian-Sudanese machinery to review the progress of the Sudanese towards self-government.[3] The same proposal regarding this

---

[1] From a statement made to the Legislative Assembly by the Civil Secretary on behalf of the Governor-General on 25th October, 1951.

[2] House of Commons Debates, 5th Series, Vol. 493, cols. 1176–1178.

[3] See above p. 118.

tripartite committee was agreed upon by the British Ambassador in Cairo and the Egyptian Foreign Secretary in 1948 but was rejected by the Foreign Relations Committee of the Egyptian Senate. The third attempt was made by Mr. Herbert Morrison when he presented the following proposals on 14th October, 1951, to the Egyptian Government just before they abrogated the 1936 Treaty and the 1899 Agreements. The proposals are quoted in full because, in the opinion of the writer, which will be expressed later, they form the basis for a satisfactory settlement if certain amendments could be introduced.

(a) An international Commission to reside in the Sudan to watch over the constitutional development of the country, and to tender advice to the Co-Domini. The Commission would include representatives of the Co-Domini: and the U.S.A. would be invited to join. Sudanese representation would not be debarred, and the proposal for the setting up of this International Commission would be subject to the agreement of the Sudanese.

(b) A joint Anglo-Egyptian statement of common principle with regard to the Sudan.

(c) An international guarantee of Nile Waters agreements.

(d) Establishment of a Nile Waters Development Authority to develop the Nile, possibly with assistance from the International Bank.

(e) An agreed date to be fixed for the attainment of self-government by the Sudanese as a first step on the way to the choice by the Sudanese of their final status.

Reference (b) above, His Britannic Majesty's Government has suggested four principles which might serve as a basis for a joint Anglo-Egyptian statement of common principle.

These are:

(a) In view of the dependence of both Egypt and the Sudan on the waters of the Nile and in order to ensure the fullest co-operation in expanding the supplies available and in sharing them, it is essential that the friendliest relations should link the two peoples.

(b) It is the common aim of Egypt and Great Britain to enable the people of the Sudan to attain full self-government as soon as possible and thereafter choose freely for themselves their form of government and the relationship with Egypt that will best meet their needs as they then exist.

(c) In view of the wide differences of culture, race, religion and political development existing among the Sudanese, the process of attaining full self-government requires the co-operation of Egypt and the United Kingdom with the Sudanese.

(d) The two Governments therefore agree to set up forthwith an International Commission in order to help the Sudanese towards the goal in (b) and to assist them in formulating their future Constitution.[1]

The British settlement has much to be said for it from the point of view of international law and from that of the principles of the United Nations. The difficulty that stands in its way as a practical settlement is that Egypt and the pro-Egyptian elements in the Sudan never had any confidence in it. They suspect that it is a policy which aims at giving the Sudan a status which will serve British rather than Egyptian and Sudanese interests. They believe that the Sudanese people will never be able to exercise their choice freely because the Sudan is administered by the British, who will remain in the country while it is being prepared for self-government and, when the time for self determination comes, they will strongly influence the choice of the Sudanese.

Had Britain and Egypt agreed on something on the lines of the proposals submitted by Mr. Morrison a satisfactory settlement would have been reached. But since they have not agreed the British policy, unilaterally enforced by the British Government, is very likely to meet with opposition and boycotting. The result, as mentioned above, will be the widening of the chasm between those who believe in independence and those who want a form of unity with Egypt in the Sudan. This may ultimately lead to much more serious results than the teething troubles which the Sudan is bound to face in its early years of nationhood.

Finally, a settlement which is favoured by some Sudanese is placing the Sudan under the international Trusteeship System. Since the Sudan is not held by Britian and Egypt under mandate

---

[1] Issued as a Communiqué by the Public Relations Office of the Sudan Government in Khartoum on 15th October, 1951.

and since it is not a territory which has been detached from enemy states as a result of the Second World War, it cannot be taken over by the Trusteeship Council unless both Great Britain and Egypt agree under Article 77 (c) of the Charter voluntarily to place it under the trusteeship system.

This may be a satisfactory settlement and the writer has reason to believe that the Sudanese, especially the educated classes, would welcome such a step. When Mr. Morrison's proposals were made public the international commission which he suggested was mistaken for a United Nations Commission and was therefore very favourably received by those classes. The difficulty, of course, is that Great Britain and Egypt may not agree to hand the Sudan over. The British have shown their resentment to the 'interference' of the Special Committee appointed by the United Nations as a result of Article 73 (e)[1] in the affairs of their colonies. Egypt, in view of her vital interests in the Sudan and considering the unanimous support given by all her parties to the 'Sudan Decree' showed herself, up to the time of the abrogation of the 1899 Agreements, even more reluctant than Britain to place the Sudan under international trusteeship.

The writer believes that the main principles laid down in Mr. Morrison's proposals cover all the essential requirements for a fair settlement. They guarantee for the Sudanese their rights of self-government and self-determination. They state, for the first time, the British Government's willingness to fix a date for the attainment of self-government and consequently of self determination, a promise which will dispel all suspicions about British sincerity; they safeguard their interests in the Nile waters; they stress the importance of close and friendly relations with Egypt with which the Sudan is naturally more closely related than it is with any other country; and they accept the principle of international

---

[1] Article 73 (e) reads: To transmit regularly to the Secretary-General for information purposes, subject to such limitation as security and constitutional considerations may require, statistical and other information of technical nature relating to economic social, and educational conditions in the territories for which they (Members of the United Nations which have or assume responsibilities for the administration of dependent territories) are respectively responsible other than those territories to which Chapters XII and XIII apply (i.e. Trust Territories).

supervision over the advancement of the Sudan towards self-government.

The proposals also guarantee for Egypt her legitimate rights in the Nile waters and accept the idea of unity of the Nile valley provided the Sudanese decide in favour of it when they come to determine their future status. They accept the principle of international supervision which Egypt desires to serve as a safeguard against the influence exerted over Sudanese opinion by British administrators.

Mr. Morrison's proposals and the statement made by Mr. Eden in the House of Commons on 15th November, 1951, go all the way to meet the proposals made by Mohammed Salah ed Din Pasha, the Egyptian Foreign Secretary, to the British Ambassador in Cairo in December, 1950, and in July, 1951. The agreed minutes of the discussions published in Cairo[1] and in a White Paper[2] published in London on 29th November, 1951, show that the Egyptian Foreign Minister suggested a two-year transition period during which the Sudan should be prepared for self-government and for a plebiscite about its future status.

If a satisfactory arrangement could be reached about the supervision of Sudanese self-government and the plebiscite it could be said that the British proposals had become identical with those put forward by Egypt and that complete agreement had been reached.

In the opinion of the writer, however, some amendments should be made in the British plan to meet not only Egyptian criticisms but those of the pro Egyptian elements in the Sudan and of some independent opinion in the country. These concern the method of the appointment and the composition of the international commission which is to reside in the Sudan and to supervise its advance towards self-government and to conduct the plebiscite. The commission should be appointed by the United Nations and should consist of disinterested members. The suggestion of the United States of America by the British Government for the membership of the commission does not dispel Egyptian fears.

[1] A resumé of these was given in a letter to The Times by Jon Kimche on 7th November, 1951.

[2] Anglo-Egyptian Conversations on the Defence of the Suez Canal and on the Sudan, December, 1950–November, 1951. Cmd. 8419.

America is Britain's most important ally to-day and she is vitally concerned in the Middle East and is as much interested as Britain in the Suez Canal.

The same feeling as that of Egypt about the importance of a United Nations Commission was shown by representatives of some Sudanese parties and some independent members of the Sudanese Commission which was appointed by the Governor-General to draft a self-governing constitution for the country. All thirteen members of this commission agreed on all the articles of the draft constitution but five of them insisted upon the appointment of a supervisory United Nations Commission. When no agreement was reached on this point the five members withdrew and the British chairman of the Sudanese Commission had to advise the Governor-General to dissolve it.

The writer appreciates the difficulties and the embarrassment which might be caused to administrators who have spent their lives working in the country when they see that they are not trusted to act as referees for the people whom they trained in the last stage of their work. But, in view of the long-drawn out nature of this dispute and the misfortunes which will befall the Sudanese if it is allowed to drag on, it appears that the advantages of agreeing to such a Commission by far outweigh the disadvantages.

It is to Britain, as the more influential partner in the Condominium, that the appeal should be made to take the lead by bringing the matter to the United Nations for the appointment of a supervisory commission. When her proposals and those put forward by Salah ed Din Pasha come to be considered by the United Nations, there seems to be every hope that a settlement might be reached. The continuance of this impasse will allow frustration, restlessness and trouble to breed in the country. Great Britain has regarded the Sudan as a territory in which she has done splendid administrative work. The Sudanese appreciate this and are grateful for the high standards of justice and administration built in the last fifty years. Let this work, of which Britain is proud, be crowned with a forward policy which aims at laying equally strong foundations of internal peace. Let the far sighted policy of Mr. Attlee, which resulted in the best relations between India and the former imperial power, be extended to other peoples before these, in their craving for liberty and a place under the sun, turn their faces away from her, confirmed in the belief that she is persisting in her policy of nineteenth century imperialism.

An appeal should also be made to Egypt, the sister country, to do all she can to understand the problems and aspirations of the Sudanese. It is in the interest of both parts of the Nile valley that their peoples should live side by side in peace and contentment. The bonds of language and culture should be strengthened by a forward policy imbued with the spirit of the modern age. Egypt should not allow the Sudanese to feel that she wants to impose her will upon them or that she wants their personality to be lost in hers. Finally, she should refrain from antagonizing the freedom-loving Sudanese by branding them as traitors ready to collaborate with a power which desires to deprive their country of its freedom. There is plenty of scope for cultural and economic co-operation between the two peoples who, if peace and equality could be achieved, could go forward together in friendship.

APPENDIXES

APPENDIX A

THE ANGLO-EGYPTIAN AGREEMENT OF 1899

Agreement between Her Britannic Majesty's Government and the Government of His Highness the Khedive of Egypt, relative to the future administration of the Sudan.

WHEREAS certain provinces in the Sudan which were in rebellion against the authority of His Highness have now been reconquered by the joint military and financial efforts of Her Britannic Majesty's Government and the Government of His Highness the Khedive; and WHEREAS it has become necessary to decide upon a system for the administration of and for the making of laws for the said reconquered provinces, under which due allowance may be made for the backward and unsettled condition of large portions thereof, and for the varying requirements of different localities; and WHEREAS it is desired to give effect to the claims which have accrued to Her Britannic Majesty's Government, by right of conquest, to share in the present settlement and future working and development of the said system of administration and legislation; and WHEREAS it is conceived that for many purposes Wadi Halfa and Suakin may be most effectively administered in conjunction with the reconquered provinces to which they are respectively adjacent;

NOW IT IS HEREBY AGREED AND DECLARED by and between the undersigned, duly authorized for that purpose as follows:

ARTICLE 1

The word 'Sudan' in this agreement means all the territories south of the 22nd parallel of latitude, which—

1. Have never been evacuated by Egyptian troops since the year 1882; or

2. Which, having before the late rebellion been administered by the Government of His Highness the Khedive, were temporarily lost to Egypt, and have been reconquered by Her Majesty's

Government and the Egyptian Government, acting in concert; or

3. Which may be hereafter reconquered by the two Governments acting in concert.

ARTICLE II

The British and Egyptian flags shall be used together, both on land and water, throughout the Sudan, except in the town of Suakin,[1] in which locality the Egyptian flag alone shall be used.

ARTICLE III

The supreme military and civil command of the Sudan shall be vested in one officer, termed the 'Governor-General of the Sudan'. He shall be appointed by Khedivial Decree on the recommendation of her Britannic Majesty's Government and shall be removed only by Khedivial Decree, with the consent of Her Britannic Majesty's Government.

ARTICLE IV

Laws, as also orders and regulations with the full force of law, for the good government of the Sudan, and for regulating the holding, disposal, and devolution of property of every kind therein situate, may from time to time be made, altered, or abrogated by Proclamation of the Governor-General. Such laws, orders, and regulations may apply to the whole or any named part of the Sudan, and may, either explicitly or by necessary implication, alter or abrogate any existing law or regulation.

All such Proclamations shall be forthwith notified to Her Britannic Majesty's Agent and Consul-General in Cairo, and to the President of the Council of Ministers of His Highness the Khedive.

ARTICLE V

No Egyptian law, decree, ministerial arrete, or other enactment hereafter to be made or promulgated shall apply to the Sudan or any part thereof, save in so far as the same shall be applied by Proclamation of the Governor-General in manner hereinbefore provided.

---

[1] A separate agreement was signed about Suakin on the 19th January, 1899 but was repealed in July of the same year and the administration of the town became the same as the rest of the country.

ARTICLE VIII

The jurisdiction of the Mixed Tribunals shall not extend nor be recognized for any purpose whatsoever, in any part of the Sudan, except in the town of Suakin.

ARTICLE IX

Until and save so far as it shall be otherwise determined by Proclamation, the Sudan with the exception of Suakin shall be and remain under martial law.

ARTICLE X

No Consuls, Vice-Consuls, or Consular Agents, shall be accredited in respect of nor allowed to reside in the Sudan, without the previous consent of Her Britannic Majesty's Government.

ARTICLE XI

The importation of slaves into the Sudan, as also their exportation, is absolutely prohibited. Provision shall be made by Proclamation for the enforcement of this regulation.

ARTICLE XII

It is agreed between the two Governments that special attention shall be paid to the Brussels Act of the 2nd July, 1890 in respect to the import, sale, and manufacture of firearms and their munitions, and distilled, or spirituous liquors.

Done in Cairo, the 19th January, 1899.

(Signed) BOUTROS GHALI.
CROMER.

APPENDIX B

LORD CROMER'S MEMORANDUM TO THE SEC-
RETARY OF STATE FOR FOREIGN AFFAIRS SUPPORT-
ING HIS DRAFT OF THE ANGLO-EGYPTIAN AGREE-
MENT ON THE SUDAN.[1]

No. 1.

(Lord Cromer to the Marquess of Salisbury—Received November
20, 1898).

(Separate and Secret)

Cairo November 10, 1898.

My Lord,

For some while past I have been discussing the question of the
future political status of the Soudan with the various Authorities
in Cairo, and I have now the honour to inclose the draft of an
Agreement with the Egyptian Government, together with an
explanatory Memorandum.

I have mentioned to the President of the Egyptian Council and
to the Minister for Foreign Affairs that some agreement of this
sort will be necessary. So far as I can gather from what they let
fall in conversation, they fully agree in the general principles
involved. I have, however, not attempted to discuss the details
with them. Some opposition from the Khedive is, I presume, to
be anticipated.

I venture to suggest that the Sirdar, who is now in England,
should be consulted on this subject.

Your Lordship will observe that Article 6 of the proposed
Agreement raises a financial question. For the rest, most of the
points involved are mainly legal and political.

From the point of view of the Administration of the Soudan, it is
on many grounds desirable that the question now raised should
be settled with as little delay as possible. Whether its consideration

[1] It is not considered necessary to give the text of Lord Cromer's draft agreement.
Some amendments and changes were made in the draft and the result was the Agreement given in Appendix A. The aim of reproducing this memorandum is to show the
arguments on which the Agreement was based.

should be postponed in view of the issues which have arisen in respect to the Upper Nile between the English and French Governments is a point on which I am unable to express any opinion.

I have, &c.,

(Signed) Cromer.

Inclosure 1 in No. 1.

MEMORANDUM

(Confidential)

It is becoming a matter of much importance to settle the future political status of the Soudan. I have carefully considered whether it would not be possible to allow matters to drift on, and to settle each point of difficulty on its own merits as it comes up for solution. If we only had to deal with the natives of the Soudan, much might be said in favour of the adoption of this course. The purely native requirements are, in fact, very simple.

A light system of taxation, some very simple forms for the administration of civil and criminal justice, and the appointment of a few carefully selected officials with a somewhat wide discretionary power to deal with local details, are all that for the time being is necessary. Gradually, as was done in what used to be called 'non-Regulation' provinces in India, a more regular and complex system could be substituted for the somewhat patriarchal forms of Government which, for the present, would suffice to meet the circumstances of the case.

We have, however, not merely to deal with the natives of the Soudan. Numerous demands have been received from Europeans who wish to reside, to invest capital, to trade with and to acquire real property in the country. It is obviously both impossible to exclude them and undesirable to do so, for without European capital and assistance no real progress can be made. One of the main difficulties of the situation, therefore, consists in the very marked contrast between the primitive institutions which, for the time being at all events, are alone suitable to the native population, and the more complex administrative and judicial machinery which the presence of the Europeans in the country will in some degree necessitate. Under these circumstances, we shall, I think, be obliged to some extent to fall back, for awhile at all events, on the argument that if Europeans choose to trade with, or reside in, a country only just emerging from barbarism, they must rest content with the best judicial and administrative institutions that the Government can give them; and the best will certainly be, for the time being, defective if judged not merely by a European, but by an Egyptian standard. It is possible that some special Court will have to be eventually created for the trial of civil and criminal affairs in which Europeans are interested. I need not, however, dwell on this point now. It is one which will require very careful consideration before any action is taken. The question which demands more immediate treatment is somewhat different. It is how by timely action to prevent the acquisition of rights and the recognition of privileges to Europeans similar to the rights and privileges which exist in Egypt. I cannot but think that if we allow Europeans to trade with, and, still more, to reside and to hold real property in, the Soudan without some distinct declaration of the general political, administrative, and judicial regime which is for the future to exist in that country, we shall be laying the seeds of much future trouble. It is only just as politic that Europeans should have some foreknowledge of what they have to expect. In default of any authoritative declaration they may not unnaturally consider, and many of them will certainly consider, that the status of Europeans resident in the Soudan is similar to that which obtains in Egypt.

On these grounds, as well as for the reason that, from a political point of view, it would seem desirable from the outset to define the British position in the Soudan with as great precision as is possible, I venture to think that some public act laying down the political status of the Soudan is necessary.

What, therefore, is the political status of the country to be? Annexation by England would, of course, solve all the difficulties of which I am now treating. But I understand that, for many obvious political and financial reasons, we do not wish to annex. On the other hand, the recognition of the Soudan as a portion of the Ottoman dominions, in no way distinct from the rest of Egypt, would perpetuate all the international difficulties and obstruction of which, during the last fifteen years, we have had such an unfortunate experience in dealing with Egyptian affairs. Under these circumstances, we have to find a compromise between the two extremes. Such a compromise may, I think, be found; but it is to be remembered that we shall be creating a status hitherto unknown to the law of Europe, and that, therefore—more especially in view of the extreme complication of some of the details—it is no easy matter to put down on paper any arrangement which may confidently be predicted to be workable in practice, and perfectly capable of defence in all its parts by valid and logical argument.

I think the arrangement had better take the form of a Convention or Agreement with the Egyptian Government.

The validity of any such Convention may, and, without doubt, will be challenged.

In the first place, it may be argued that, under the Imperial Firmans, the Khedive has no right to make any Treaty with a foreign power other than Commercial and Customs Conventions, and those which concern the relations of foreigners with the internal administration of the country.

Moreover, it is laid down in the Firman to the present Khedive that he 'shall not, on any pretext or motive, abandon to others, in whole or in part, the privileges accorded to Egypt, which are intrusted to him, and which pertain to the inherent rights of the Sovereign Power, nor any portion of the territory'.

To arguments based on these considerations a twofold answer may be given.

In the first place, it may be said that the Convention is no Treaty properly so called; that in signing it the Khedive will not perform any act of external sovereignty; that he will merely be exercising his acknowledged right of making arrangements for the internal administration of the territory accorded to him by the Firmans; and that the fact of the Egyptian flag continuing, in concert with the British, to fly everywhere in the Soudan, shows that the suzerainty of the Sultan is, in part at all events, still recognized in that country.

This argument is, however, in my opinion, weak, for the more we dwell on whatever fragment of the Sultan's suzerainty which will remain, the more difficult will it be to differentiate the Soudan from the rest of the Ottoman dominion in respect to the treatment of Europeans and other subjects.

I prefer, therefore, to take our stand boldly on the second argument, and that is that the Egyptian army, which forms part of the Ottoman army, was unable to maintain its position in the Soudan, and would unaided have been quite unable to reconquer that country; that the reconquest has been effected by English money, English troops, and Egyptian troops officered and trained by Englishmen; that this fact confers on Her Majesty's Government, on the recognized principles of international law, predominant rights in the determination of the future regime of the country; that the question of whether the Khedive is acting within his rights is therefore beside the mark, for that, rather than ceding anything to England, he is obtaining concessions from England.

I now proceed to offer some explanatory remarks on the various Articles of the draft Convention annexed to this Memorandum.

Preamble.—In the preamble allusion is made incidentally and inferentially to the rights of the Khedive anterior to the Mahdist rebellion, but more prominence is given to the rights of the British Government accruing from the fact of the reconquest. It appears necessary to state these rights, as they alone constitute the real justification for the creation of a political and administrative status in the Soudan different to that which exists in Egypt.

Article I.—This Article gives a definition of the territories which, for the purposes of the present Convention, will be comprised, in the Soudan. I should mention, by way of explanation, that the 22nd parallel of latitude runs a few miles north of Wady Halfa. Suakin is well south of this line.

If we wish to be perfectly consistent with the principles more or less explicitly set forth in the preamble, the term 'Soudan' should be strictly limited to the territories which formerly belonged to Egypt, which were subsequently held by the Dervishes, and which, at one time or another, have been reconquered with British assistance. To do this, however, will create great administrative inconvenience, for we shall then have to exclude Suakin and Wady Halfa from the Soudan. Neither of these towns has ever been occupied by the Dervishes, although it would be perfectly correct as a matter of fact to say that, but for the defensive action taken from time to time by British troops and under British auspices, they would certainly have been lost to Egypt during the rebellion.

It will be observed that in this Article the territories comprised in the Soudan are divided into three categories. These are:—

1. Those 'which have never been evacuated by Egyptian troops since the year 1882'. This formula has been adopted in order to include Wady Halfa and Suakin.

2. Those 'which, having before the late rebellion in the Soudan been administered by the Government of his Highness the Khedive, were temporarily lost to Egypt and have been reconquered by Her Majesty's Government and the Egyptian Government acting in concert'. Under this heading will be included all the territory recently reconquered. There is an objection to saying 'all the territory which formerly belonged to Egypt' (or words to that effect) without any limitation as to reconquest by an Anglo-Egyptian force, as the use of these words might be held to include part of the Equatorial Province and even possibly Zeyla and Berbera, which, of course, are not intended to be included in the present Agreement.

3. Those 'which may hereafter be reconquered by the two Governments acting in concert'. This provision has been so worded as to include extensions southwards or westwards, acquired by Anglo-Egyptian action, and at the same time to exclude extensions from Uganda northwards, made by the English Government acting alone.

Article II.—At the present the English and the Egyptian flags are flying together at Khartoum. It is now proposed, in order to indicate that the political status of the whole Soudan is to be the same, to adopt a similar measure throughout the whole country, except at Suakin.

It would raise a great outcry to hoist the British flag at Suakin, and it is really hardly necessary to do so. As I shall presently explain, it is proposed to make a difference between Suakin and the rest of the Soudan in respect to the jurisdiction of the Mixed Tribunals.

Articles III and IV may conveniently be considered together.

They are in some respects the most important portions of the proposed Convention. They regulate the manner in which both the supreme legislative and executive authority in the Soudan shall be exercised.

1. It is proposed to vest the supreme military and civil command in the hands of one officer, who will be termed the 'Governor-General of the Soudan'. Of the desirability of this measure there can, I conceive, be little doubt. It is suggested that he should be appointed 'by Khedivial Decree on the recommendation of Her Majesty's Government'. This is much the same formula as is adopted in the case of nominating the Commissioners of the Debt and some other officials. I should add that I should prefer that allusion should be specifically made in the preamble of the Decree to the fact that English sanction has been obtained to the nomination, though the adoption of this course is not altogether necessary, for the Khedive is under an obligation to follow English advice in all important matters so long as the occupation lasts.

2. It is proposed that all Proclamations issued by the Governor-General shall have the force of law, but that, in respect to all important matters, the previous consent of the Khedive, 'acting under the advice of his Council of Ministers',[1] and of the British Government, acting through their Representatives, should be obtained. It is obviously necessary that the Governor-General should be under some control, and the only really effective control will be that of the English Government acting through their Consul-General; but the Khedive must also be mentioned, both because, *ex hypothesi*, the Soudan, though possessing a separate political status, is still to be Egyptian territory, and because the financial responsibilities assumed by Egypt render it both necessary and desirable that the voice of the Egyptian Government should be heard.

Whether, in the case of each Proclamation, it should be stated that the British and Egyptian consent has been obtained is an open question. I do not think the adoption of this procedure absolutely

---

[1] It is not absolutely necessary to introduce this phrase, as, under Ismail Pasha's Rescript of August, 1878, the Khedive is always supposed to act under the advice of his Council of Ministers, but, inasmuch as the Khedive constantly endeavours to escape from this obligation, I think it would be advisable to allude to the point.

necessary, and perhaps it would be as well to do whatever is possible to make the Governor-General absolutely supreme in the eyes of the population of the Soudan.

3. Although, as I have already said, it is necessary that some effective control should be exercised over the action of the Governor-General, it would be a great mistake to centralize the administration of the Soudan in the hands of any authority, British or Egyptian, at Cairo. It is proposed, therefore, to take power in the Convention to dispense with the previous assent of the Khedive and of the English Diplomatic Agent in certain matters. The detailed points in respect to which a free hand shall be left to the Governor-General can form the subject of subsequent discussion.

Article V.—This Article deals with the body of laws which shall be applicable in the Soudan.

In the course of the discussions which have taken place here, it was at first proposed that no Egyptian law should be valid in the Soudan unless it had been specially applied to that country by Proclamation of the Governor-General. The objection to this course is that, for the time being—that is to say, until a body of laws can be framed for the Soudan—there would be a condition of complete lawlessness. It has been thought better, therefore, to allow such Egyptian legislation as may, on legal principles, be held to be in force in the Soudan, to hold good. I am advised that, on the legal principle applicable to the case, only Egyptian legislation previous to the year 1884—the first year in which the Soudan fell completely under Dervish control—is legally in force in the Soudan. This would include the Egyptian Codes as promulgated in June 1883. At the same time it is proposed to limit the application of all future Egyptian laws to Egypt proper, unless they are specially applied to the Soudan. It will be borne in mind that under Article IV all existing Egyptian laws may be altered or abrogated by Proclamation of the Governor-General.

Article VI.—This article deals with the important question of finance.

It is obviously undesirable that the Caisse de la Dette should be allowed to interfere in Soudan affairs, but after fully discussing this matter with Mr. Gorst, I have come to the conclusion that it would be best to make no allusion to this subject in the Convention. As matters at present stand, the net charge on account of the Soudan appears on the expenditure side of the Egyptian accounts. To this arrangement the Caisse has agreed. No question can, therefore, arise with the Caisse until the Soudan yields a surplus of revenue over expenditure, and if—as a mere matter of account—we charge as much as possible to the Soudan, as it will be to our interest to do, a long time will elapse before any real surplus accrues. Moreover, should any difficulties arise with the Caisse, I doubt whether any provision made in this Agreement will much help towards a settlement. On the whole, therefore, I think we had better leave this branch of the question alone for the present.

Turning to another point—it is proposed that the whole of the Soudan revenue shall be placed at the disposal of the Egyptian Government, and that, on the other hand, that Government shall be 'solely responsible for the civil and ordinary military expenditure'.

So far as I can yet see, the Soudan figures work out much more favourably than I anticipated. I have no doubt that the Egyptian Treasury will be able to bear all the ordinary expenditure, civil and military, without making any call for British assistance.

On the other hand, it will be observed that the Article now under discussion contains the following provision:—

'Her Britannic Majesty's Government undertakes to bear the whole cost of any British troops who may be stationed in the Soudan other than special expeditionary forces.'

Both Sir Francis Grenfell and Lord Kitchener are strongly of opinion that a small British force of, say, two companies, or about 250 men, should be permanently stationed at Khartoum. I entirely agree with them. Their presence will give confidence to every one, and will be a very useful counterpoise in the event of any difficulties occurring with native, notably the black, troops.

I cannot at present say what would be the extra expenditure involved, but it will certainly be a small sum, more especially as the two companies can be detached from Cairo, without increasing the total British force in Egypt.

I earnestly hope that Her Majesty's Government will consent to bear this small charge. It would produce a very bad effect were I to ask the Egyptian Government for the money. Moreover, under all the circumstances of the case, it would seem to me a fair charge on the English Treasury.

Lastly, I do not in any way anticipate that the necessity of sending any further expeditionary force to the Soudan will arise. Should, however, anything of the kind unfortunately occur, the division of cost between England and Egypt may, I think, best be settled at the time, and according to the special circumstances of the case. Hence the last paragraph in Article VI.

Article VII.—In this Article the right to lay down the conditions under which Europeans shall trade with, reside in, or hold property in the Soudan, is asserted. For the reasons which I have already stated, this right will almost certainly be contested. This is unfortunate, but it cannot be helped. We are in possession, and shall be able to assert our rights, even although we may not be able to convince others of the regularity of our position, or the validity of our arguments. In the meanwhile, we may perhaps do something towards mitigating hostility if we proclaim the commercial policy now known as that of the 'open door', and if we state that in all other respects Europeans, of whatsoever nationality, will be treated alike.

Article VIII.—This article deals with the question of customs duties.

I should explain briefly what is the present Egyptian regime in these matters.

Under the Imperial Firmans, the Khedive has a right to make Commercial Conventions with other Powers. As a matter of fact, during the last few years such Conventions have been concluded with England, Germany, Austria, Italy, and some of the minor Powers; but, inasmuch as a provision common to all these Conventions is that they shall not come into force unless Conventions have been signed with all the Powers, and inasmuch as France, Russia, and some other Powers have concluded no Conventions, the whole of the Conventions signed by the Egyptian Government are at present inoperative. Customs duties in Egypt are, therefore, at present levied exclusively under the Conventions existing between Turkey and the various European Powers. Under these circumstances, an *ad valorem* import duty of eight per cent and an export duty of one per cent are levied.

The proposed Article VIII is conceived, in a sense, from which the right to separate the commercial regime of the Soudan from that of Egypt may be inferred, even if it be not expressly stated. As in other similar cases, this right will, of course, be contested, and we must again fall back on the right of conquest argument.

As a matter of fact, however, I do not propose that any extra import duty should be levied on goods entering the Soudan from Egypt, or from any of the ports of the Red Sea, which will now be comprised in the term 'Soudan'. On the other hand, care has been taken to draft Article VIII in such a manner as to preserve complete liberty of action in respect to trade entering the Soudan, not from Egypt or the Red Sea, but from other directions.

The export duties stand on a somewhat different footing. It may become necessary and desirable to impose a higher duty than one per cent on some articles, such as gum and ostrich feathers. It is proposed, therefore, to maintain our liberty of action on that point.

Article IX.—This article lays down that the jurisdiction of the Mixed Courts will not be recognized anywhere in the Soudan, except in the town of Suakin.

In connection with this subject, I append to this Memorandum two documents prepared by Mr. McIlwraith, from which it appears that some doubt exists as to whether, even supposing no change to be made in the political status of the Soudan, the jurisdiction of the Mixed Courts extends to that country. The decisions of the Court of Appeal on this subject have been contradictory. For my own part, I may say that the balance of argument seems to me decidedly in favour of the view that the Mixed Courts have no jurisdiction. However this may be, it must be remembered that the tendency of the Courts is to extend their jurisdiction, that they practically are under no legislative control, and that, if they assume jurisdiction over the Soudan, the only means of resisting their encroachments is to refuse to serve their writs or execute their judgements. I think, therefore, it would be advisable not to rely on the arguments adduced by Mr. McIlwraith, which are based on the original Charter of Organization and cognate considerations, but to fall back again on the special political status of the Soudan as the main reason for refusing to admit the jurisdiction of the Courts.

It will be observed that it is proposed to exempt Suakin from the operation of this Article. Rightly or wrongly, the jurisdiction of the Mixed Courts at Suakin has for many years past been recognized. It would raise a great outcry to make any change, neither do I think that any change is much required. I am inclined, therefore, to leave matters alone in respect to this special point.

Article X.—This Article provides that, for the time being, martial law shall prevail in the Soudan, except in the town of Suakin.

I am advised that, for reasons which are familiar to all who have studied this question, 'martial' and not 'military', law is the proper term to use in this connection.

I may remark incidentally that the proclamation of martial law will strengthen our case as regards declining to admit the jurisdiction of the Mixed Courts, for I conceive that many Judges, who would refuse to admit the validity of our rights based on reconquest, would recognize that, so long as the ordinary civil law was in abeyance, the Courts could exercise no jurisdiction.

It is not, however, mainly on this account that I advocate the proclamation of martial law. I do so because, for the time being, I think that the adoption of this course is necessitated by the state of the country. It is still very disturbed. I hear of frequent cases of brigandage. Under the circumstances, I think that very ample powers for the maintenance of order must be vested in the hands of the Governor-General. Notably, he should have the right of expelling any individual, European or native, from the country.

I should add that the proclamation of martial law does not necessarily imply that all matters are to be settled by the simple order of the Governor-General, or of some military officer to whom he may have delegated his powers. Law Courts, the nature of which I need not now describe in detail, have been already instituted in the Dongola Province. They appear to be working fairly well. Provision has been made in the Soudan Budget for an extension of these institutions. The spirit, therefore, in which I propose the proclamation of martial law is this: that the extreme powers which will thus be vested in the Governor-General shall only be used in exceptional cases; and, further, that, as time goes on, every endeavour shall be made to bring the administration of the law in the Soudan into harmony with the general recognized principles of civil jurisprudence.

Article XI.—This Article provides that no Consular authorities are to reside in the Soudan without the permission of Her Majesty's Government. This seems to me to be necessary, but our right to make this provision will, of course, be challenged by those who hold that the political status of the Soudan in no way differs from that of other parts of Ottoman dominions.

Article XII.—I think we may at once go so far as to forbid the importation and exportation of slaves into and from the Soudan. The question of how to deal with domestic slavery in the Soudan is much more difficult. For the moment we had better leave it alone.

Article XIII.—Although such a course is not absolutely necessary, it may perhaps be as well to draw special attention to the provisions of the Brussels Act as regards the sale and importation of arms and spirituous liquors.[1]

Cairo, November 10, 1898.   (Signed) CROMER.

---

[1] F. O. 78/4957.

APPENDIX C

THE SOUTHERN SUDAN [1]

Reference was made in the Chapter on the Country and the People to the problem of the Southern Sudan. It is a problem which, in many respects, has a number of parallels in Africa and Asia as well as in Europe. It arose in history whenever territorial boundaries came to be drawn in places where racial, cultural, religious and historical considerations were among the deciding factors. Indeed, the boundary between Egypt herself and the Sudan has been the subject of the controversy between Egypt and Great Britain on the one hand and between Egypt and the Sudanese on the other.

As was already mentioned the problem of the relations between the northern and southern parts of the Sudan never became an issue in the dispute between Egypt and Britain. It was considered for a long time as an internal problem of administration. This is why it was not discussed earlier in the book. But later developments in the Sudan Government's 'Southern Policy' drove the writer and many other Sudanese into the great suspicion that the aim of the 'Southern Policy' was to separate the south from the north and add it to British East Africa or turn it into a Pakistan. It is therefore necessary to discuss this problem in some greater detail.

In order to meet the geographical and political difficulties explained in the introductory chapter [2] the Sudan Government formulated a special administrative policy for the south which had the professed aim of protecting the southerner from exploitation by the northerner. [3] This aim was clear, and, as long as any real danger of any form of exploitation by the north existed, it was understandable and morally justified. But its ultimate aims remained a guarded secret until 1947. In this year an official document ———— The Sudan, A Record of Progress 1898-1947 ————

[1] See reference to this subject in the Editor's Preface, p. xi.
[2] See above pp. 18–19.
[3] See above p. 19.

was released just before the Security Council started to hear Egypt's case against the British position in the Sudan. After mentioning the fears of the northern Sudanese that the final object of the 'Southern Policy' might be to split the country in half and even to attach the south or part of it to Uganda, the document tells us, 'The arguments whether such a course would be to the ultimate advantage of the Southern Sudan or to the rest of Africa are many on both sides and the whole question might at some date form a proper subject for consideration by an international commission.'[1] No definite goal of the policy is given in this passage but it shows clearly that the Sudan Government had their doubts on the propriety of a united Sudan and preferred to see a recommendation on the ultimate future of the south made by an international body. But their attitude was made clearer in the next paragraph which said, 'Meanwhile, the present Government . . . while doing nothing to prejudice the issue, is proposing to associate sympathetic northern Sudanese with the implementation of a policy which aims at giving the south the same chances of ultimate self-determination as have been promised to the north.'[2] Not only does this passage confirm the doubts about a united Sudan implied in the previous one, but it tells us that the ultimate aim of the 'Southern Policy' is to prepare the south for self-determination.

However, a change of policy took place in 1948 when the Governor-General in Council, with the support of the British Government, passed the Executive Council and Legislative Assembly Ordinance which provides for the representation of the three southern provinces on the Legislative Assembly before which comes all government legislation for the whole country.

The association of the southerners with the northerners in the government of a united Sudan was recommended by the Sudan Administration Conference, which was appointed by the Governor-General to make recommendations on the steps which should follow the Advisory Council for the Northern Sudan towards self-government.[3] The same recommendation was later

---

[1] Sudan Government, *The Sudan, A Record of Progress, op. cit.*, pp. 13–14.
[2] *Ibid*, p. 14.
[3] The writer was a member of this Conference.

accepted by the southern Sudanese who were invited to the Juba Conference held by the Civil Secretary of the Sudan Government in June, 1947 to ascertain the wishes of the representatives of the south. Southern Sudanese became members of the all Sudan Assembly and have dispelled the misgivings of those who feared they were politically far behind the northerners.

A further important step towards the cultural unification of the north and south was taken by the Executive Council and Legislative Assembly in 1950. A decision was made to introduce the teaching of Arabic in all government schools and in all private and mission schools above the elementary level. Southerners qualified for higher education started to go to Gordon Memorial College in Khartoum rather than to Makerere College in Uganda. These measures were first recommended by a Committee of the Sudan Administration Conference who considered that it was only when a uniform system of education was spread that a common outlook and a common feeling of citizenship could be brought about.

Although the new orientations in the policy of the Sudan Government point towards a unified Sudan, the problem of the South may yet be a subject for reconsideration when a final settlement of the future status of the Sudan comes to be made. There are some British officials in the Sudan and some men and women in England who take interest in Sudanese affairs who still have doubts about a united Sudan. The problem, therefore, deserves some discussion.

But it is important, before discussing the problem, to make some reference to the missionary societies working in the South whose activities and unfriendly attitude towards the north have accentuated the division between north and south created by the geographical and political difficulties described earlier. Christian missionary societies of various kinds began to establish themselves in the south immediately after the conquest of the Sudan in 1898. These societies, in addition to their religious and medical work, established their own schools which, until 1927, were free from government supervision and control. From 1927 onwards, because a regular system of subsidies was introduced, the mission schools came under the supervision of the Education Department. Later the Government, while continuing to subsidize and supervise an increasing number of mission schools, set up its own educational system. The missions, not unnaturally, saw in the religion and the language of the north a challenge to their activities. They therefore took every opportunity in their teaching of religion and history to keep the memory of slavery alive. The writer was given much information on this by southern friends who were educated in mission schools, and he saw at a missionary station how a huge tree, underneath which the Arabs of the north were alleged to have had their slave dealings, was carefully looked after. The improvement in the means of communications and the new orientations in the constitutional and educational fields are causing much alarm to these societies. They see in them the greatest challenge to their work. This alarm is clearly expressed in a pamphlet issued by the Church Missionary Society.[1] 'To-day', the pamphlet says, 'A channel through the *Sudd* is cut and regularly cleared. Paddle boats (the latest driven by diesel engines) maintain a fortnightly service in each direction over the thousand miles between Khartoum and Juba. More striking still is the fact that one can have tea on the airfield at Juba and be in London for lunch on the following day. The significance of this is that what prevented easy communication in the past between north and south, and between Moslem and pagan, has now disappeared; and what is a highway for Christian penetration is equally an entrance for Moslem advance and for the inflow of materialism.'[2] It also says, 'To-day the Minister for Education is a Moslem Sudanese. The Mission is already required to teach Arabic at Loka and the teaching of Arabic at all village schools is visualized in the future. It is idle to lament that greater use was not made of the opportunities of the past. Vast scope exists still for educational missionaries if they will offer their services. Closing doors should impel a sense of urgency. Every change presents its new challenge. Under the new regime and policy, boys from Loka will no longer go to Christian institutions in Uganda for higher education, but will go to university courses at the predominantly Moslem Gordon

[1] C. M. S., *The Southern Sudan Then and Now*, Adventure of Faith Series No. 12, London, 1950.
[2] *Ibid.*, p. 4.

College in Khartoum. In addition to this an increasing number of southern officials are being sent north for further training to fit them for higher posts in the several government departments. Practically all these men will be Christians in name. What a challenge there is here for them to take the Gospel of Jesus Christ to Islam, and what a challenge to us to send boys out from our schools who will be convinced, enthusiastic, and knowledgeable Christians, with a personal faith in the Living Christ which will lead them to witness fearlessly in life and speech, cost what it may.'[1] And, finally, it says, after describing the position of the southerners in the new constitutional structure, 'Although the senior British Officials who are now members of the Assembly and the Executive Council (Cabinet) will have much influence at first, there is no saying what the Assembly will do when it has found its feet. . . . The Christian members have a hard and important task. Nearly all the others are Moslems, some of them intensely bent on spreading their faith. It requires only a little knowledge and imagination to guess at the pressure and strain that will arise, especially after Sudanese independence is secured.'[2]

What are the arguments for a Southern Sudan being governed as a separate entity or being incorporated in Uganda or in a united East Africa?

The main argument put forward by the Sudan Government in defence of its policy is that the confidence of the southerners in all foreign peoples including the British administrators, which has been completely shattered by the slave trade, 'could only be won by building up a protective barrier against northern merchants'.[3] This policy, if its sole aim was the protection of the southerners, was perfectly justified so long as there was a wish on the part of the northerners to enslave the southerners, or so long as public opinion in the north remained sympathetic or indifferent when isolated cases of kidnapping took place. But there can be no justification for a policy of barriers or dismemberment when the danger of slavery has gone for ever. The Sudan is not the only place which experienced slavery and slave trade in the eighteenth

[1] *Ibid.*, pp. 12-13.
[2] *Ibid.*, p. 16.
[3] Sudan Government, *The Sudan ,A Record of Progress, op. cit.*, p. 12.

and nineteenth centuries. The greatest and most civilized countries of the world to-day, including Britain, have been guilty of
these inhuman practices on a much larger scale. Those countries
have given up the practice and none of their present day policies
towards the old homes of slaves bear any relation to the history of
slavery. The Sudanese have also gone a very long way towards
dismissing the idea of slavery and inequality among men. The
official Record of Progress itself tells us that 'the educated northerner has dismissed the idea of slavery from his mind (although he
still refuses to marry his daughter to a southerner, however Islam-
ized) but the Arab tribesman has not'.[1] That the educated northerner dismissed the idea a long time ago is very true and it is
enough to say that the most prominent political leader of the
northerners in 1924, Ali Abdel Latif, was a pure Dinka. The rapid
expansion of education in the north and the south which has been
going on will undoubtedly eradicate the idea of slavery from the
mind of every Sudanese and will bring about mutual respect.
The question of marrying daughters is a red herring in an important question like this. Marriage is a private affair and men and
women have their preferences, however homogeneous and civilized
their society may be. Northern Sudanese, Americans and British
at home and abroad need education in this matter. And if the
question of intermarriage is going to be a criterion of political
unity, then there is no hope for Kenya and similar colonies or
even for the United States.

The 'protection' argument, therefore, has only a temporary
validity. The time is quickly passing, if it has not already passed,
when it can be used to support a protection policy, let alone a
separation policy.

A second argument, which is sometimes put forward, and which
the writer heard expressed in the Sudan Administration Conference by a British member speaking in his private capacity, is
that the south lags far behind the north in political maturity.
There is some truth in the argument but it is far from being altogether true. If political advancement is measured by the incidence of education and by experience in the art of government,
then it will not be true to say that the south lags far behind the

[1] *Ibid.*, p. 13.

north. The writer prepared for the Sudan Administration Conference the figures for the incidence of elementary and inter-
mediate education from official records. The incidence of this type
of education in Equatoria (which then included Bahr-el-Ghazal)
was only second to that of the Blue Nile which includes the old
Fung Province. It is true that the incidence of higher education
was practically nil but this is being rectified by the introduction
of secondary education in the south and by sending southerners
to Gordon College. With regard to the training in the art of government the south compares favourably. Although expert opinion
does not regard the south as 'ready for fully fledged local government',[1] yet the newly constituted area councils of Bahr-el-Ghazal
'impress the visitor more than many of the fully warranted authorities of the north'.[2] The southern representatives on the Legislative
Assembly proved that they were a match for the northerners.

But even if the argument were true it is also one which has a
temporary validity and could not be used for permanent seclusion
or separation of the south.

A third argument which has not been used much, but one which
the superficial observer may be tempted to use, is the racial argument. The invalidity of this argument has been testified by the
anthropologist. It is clear from the evidence given earlier that
there are no distinct racial or cultural divisions in the Sudan,
except in small areas. Hamitic and Semitic blood and culture were
infused in the country in varying degrees and no tribe in the Sudan
can prove a pure blood or an unassimilated culture. Finally, there
is no reason why this argument which was never used for secluding
or separating the Nubians or the Beja or the tribes of Darfur and
upper Blue Nile, should be used for separating the Nilotes and
Nilo-Hamites.

The fourth argument is that of the missionary societies who
regard closer association with the north, and even the economic
development of the south, as a challenge to Christianity. Reference
was made above to their anxiety about orientations in the constitutional and educational spheres. About economic development
they say, referring to the Zande Scheme, 'In all this the infant

[1] A. H. Marshall, *Report on Local Government in the Sudan*, Khartoum, 1949, p. 32.
[2] *Ibid.*, p. 38.

Church is becoming more than a little bewildered. Can one wonder! The Church is, in fact, passing through a crisis, caused in part by this social upheaval of re-settlement, in part by the influx of money in amounts undreamed of a few years ago, and in part by the rapid change in standards. Many feel that the greatest danger to the Church to-day throughout the Sudan is from a spreading materialism . . .'[1]

It is not intended here to enter into a discussion about the truth or falsehood of Islam or Christianity, or which of them is a more suitable religion for the south. Nor is it intended to discuss whether any new religion should be preached to the pagan tribes at all. The point which should be made is that the 'iron curtain' behind which the missionary societies want the southern Sudan to continue cannot be defended. The freedom of religion is one of the freedoms for which the United Nations Charter stands, and the southern Sudanese should be given full freedom to choose the faith they want. There is no reason why the Christian missionary societies should continue to be given the protection and sponsoring which they have so far enjoyed. Their argument against another freedom for the south, freedom from want, is even less indefensible than their argument for cultural and political seclusion of that region. The Zande are a hungry people,[2] and any development which gives them, or any other tribe, more food and better conditions of life should be more than welcome. No people in the world of to-day can be kept free from cultural and economic influences. If economic development brings with it social change, as it inevitably does, it is the duty of the administrator, the educationist and the missionary to help the people they are trying to serve to go through the change with as little disturbance to their mental and spiritual peace as possible.

Whether the southern Sudanese embrace a new faith, or whether they remain pagan or turn agnostic or atheist, they can still be politically united with the north. Moslems and Christians have tolerated each other in the past and are living happily together in the modern states of the Middle East. Christians in the

---

[1] C. M. S. *The Southern Sudan Then and Now*, London, 1950, p. 11.
[2] G. M. Culwick, *A Dietary Survey Among the Zande of the South Western Sudan*, Khartoum, 1950, p. 7.

predominantly Moslem northern Sudan are living on good terms with the majority and they suffer no political or social persecution. 'Educated Sudanese,' declared the most vocal northern member of the first Legislative Assembly, 'were tolerant of other religions and had no objection to the teaching of Christianity; in fact they welcomed the missions in the Nuba Mountains and had no objection to the £E.8,003 paid to the missionaries there as subventions for educational work.'[1] The fear expressed by missionaries that the Moslem north will subjugate the south politically is, therefore, not justified.

For a united Sudan there are three main arguments. The first is that the south is financially wholly dependent on the north. The cost of administration and of the services, such as communications, the medical, educational, agricultural and other services, is borne by the north. So also is any capital and recurrent expenditure on any economic development. The initial sum voted in 1945 for the Zande Scheme, which has no aim other than improving the living conditions of that tribe was £E.500,000. The Equatoria Projects Board was authorized to spend up to £E.2,000,000. Even the missionary societies are given large subsidies to help them carry out their education in spite of the fact that the Government is launching its own ambitious programme of education. The sum allotted for these societies for the period of 18 months, January, 1950 to June, 1951, was £E.216,096. This financial liability can only be borne by the north. Even those who advocate that the south should be detached from the north are dissuaded by this fact from making a suggestion to create an independent south or to add it to Uganda. The authors of a report to the Fabian Colonial Bureau who consider that the southern Sudan belongs to Central Africa say, 'The solution however is not easy. Intensely backward in health, education, and economic development, it is at present, and possibly for ever, an economic liability to any country which accepted it and Uganda, the natural neighbour to do this, would probably refuse.'[2]

The northern Sudanese are quite willing to bear this burden,

---

[1] Mohamed Ahmed Mahgoub, *Weekly Digest of Proceedings* of the first Legislative Assembly, 22nd–28th March, 1950, p. 21.

[2] Fabian Colonial Bureau, *The Sudan, The Road Ahead*, London, 1945, pp. 25–26.

but there are many who very much suspect the ultimate aims of British policy and who argue that if a decision to separate the south is going to be forced upon them, the more quickly that decision is taken the better. The northern Sudan, they say, is a poor country and Britain, who can afford to be a philanthropist much more than the northern Sudan, should bear the burden of paying for the administration, the services and the development of the south. The British cannot justify using the money of the north on any other grounds than those of the permanent union of the two parts, and if they continue to support the south from northern funds and then decide to detach it their moral responsibility will be great.

Why are the northern Sudanese willing to support the south? Are they, as some British officials in the Sudan suggest, driven by imperialist motives? This brings us to the second argument. The northern Sudan, like Egypt, is becoming more and more dependent on the Nile for its agricultural development. And, as all the tributaries of the White Nile are in the southern Sudan, the northerners want to have those parts in their country. The reason for this is not that they want to use the water to the detriment of the south. Far from it. What they want to avoid is control by a different nation to the detriment of possible irrigation from the White Nile in the north. Secondly, they argue, that any possible agricultural development of the south, at the expense of the north, might, with the improvement of communications, turn out to be of value not only to the south, but to the country as a whole. Thirdly, many believe that the mineral wealth of that part, now an unknown quantity, might turn out to be of value to the country as a whole. The north and south might be economically complementary in the sense that the industrial south and the agricultural north might at some future date make a self-sufficing Sudan in a number of needs. This may well prove to be an illusion but it is the feeling which prevails. It is because of these reasons and not because the south is a source of cheap labour and servants, as the report to the Fabian Colonial Bureau suggests, that the northerners want the south to be united with them. The needs of cheap labour and servants are fully supplied by French Equatorial Africa and Nigeria.

Thirdly, there is the legal argument. The Sudan, in its present boundaries, was created a political entity by the 1899 Agreement. Any changes in those boundaries without the prior consent of both signatories, i.e. Egypt and Great Britain, is an infringement of international law. This argument is not a strong one because international agreements can never have permanent validity. What is a sound agreement at one time may be unsound with changing circumstances. The Sudanese themselves do not give much weight to this legal point because they, more than anybody else, feel the need for the termination of the 1899 Agreement. Their arguments for a united Sudan are related to the facts of the case rather than to legal considerations.

Such is the problem of the South and the writer sincerely hopes that, should any future event precipitate any desire for changing the policy adopted by the Governor-General in 1948, British, northern Sudanese and southern Sudanese will adopt a sane attitude and will take into consideration the facts of the case and the spirit of our age.

LIST OF BOOKS AND DOCUMENTS CONSULTED
BY THE AUTHOR

A   ORIGINAL AUTHORITIES CONSULTED

Foreign Office Records: Documents under Egypt and Turkey, 1830–1902.

Trade and Plantations Committee Report, 1789, Part VI: Trade in the Interior Parts of Africa.

C.-2395: Firmans granted by the Sultans to the Viceroys of Egypt 1841–73 with correspondence related thereto (1879).

C.-3670: Report on the Sudan by Lieutenant-Colonel Stewart (1883).

C.-3879: Correspondence respecting the Affairs of the Sudan (1884).

C.-3890: Copies of Admiralty Telegrams relative to Affairs at Suakin from 5th February to 12 February, 1884.

C.-4281: Correspondence respecting Prince Hassan's Mission to the Sudan (1885).

C.5162: Correspondence relating to claims of the Egyptian Government and counter-claims of the British Government arising from the operations in the Sudan (1887).

C.-5668: Further correspondence respecting Affairs at Suakin (1889).

C.-9054: Correspondence with the French Government respecting the valley of the Upper Nile (1898).

C.-9055: Further correspondence respecting the valley of the Upper Nile (1898).

C.-9332: Despatch from Her Majesty's Agent and Consul-General at Cairo enclosing a report on the Sudan by Sir William Garstin (1899).

CMD 1555: Papers respecting negotiations with the Egyptian delegation (1921).

CMD 1592: Correspondence respecting Affairs in Egypt (1922).

CMD 2171: Correspondence respecting the Gezira Irrigation Project (1924).

CMD 2269: Despatch to His Majesty's High Commissioner respecting the position of His Majesty's Government in regard to Egypt and the Sudan (1924).

CMD 2680: Notes Exchanged between the United Kingdom and Italy respecting Lake Tsana (1926).

CMD 3050: Papers regarding negotiations for a Treaty of Alliance with Egypt (1928).

CMD 3348: Exchange of notes between the Governments of the United Kingdom and Egypt in regard to the use of the waters of the River Nile for irrigation purposes (1929).

CMD 3376: Exchange of Notes relating to proposals for an Anglo-Egyptian Settlement (1929).

CMD 3575: Papers regarding the recent negotiations for an Anglo-Egyptian Settlement (1930).

CMD 5270, 5308: Treaty of Alliance between the United Kingdom and Egypt (1936).

CMD 5319: Agreement between His Majesty's Government in the United Kingdom and the Egyptian Government regarding Financial Questions affecting the Anglo-Egyptian Sudan (1936).

CMD 7179: Papers regarding the negotiations for a revision of the Anglo-Egyptian Treaty of 1936 (1947).

Parliamentary Debates, House of Commons—Egypt, 10th July, 1924; 23rd December, 1929; 24th November, 1936.

Reports by the Governor-General on the Administration, Finances and Conditions of the Sudan 1899–1947.

Telegram from Egyptian Prime Minister to Governor-General regarding Sudanese Nationality law (19th December, 1944).

Telegram from Governor-General to Egyptian Prime Minister regarding definition of the term Sudanese (24th December, 1944).

Letters from the Governor-General of the Sudan to British Ambassador in Cairo and Egyptian Prime Minister dated 22nd August, 1947 enclosing proposals for Legislative Assembly.

Letter from British Ambassador in Cairo to Governor-General giving British Government's approval of Legislative Assembly Proposals (23rd October, 1947).

Letter from Egyptian Prime Minister to British Foreign Secretary enclosing a note relative to Governor-General's proposals for Legislative Assembly—copy to Governor-General (26th November, 1947).

Letter from Governor-General to Egyptian Prime Minister answering criticisms contained in his note sent under letter dated 26th November, 1947 (5th January, 1948).

Official Communiqué giving Amendments to draft Legislative Assembly Ordinance made by joint Anglo-Egyptian Committee in Cairo—May, 1948.

Graduates General Congress Memorandum to the Governor-General (3rd April, 1942).

Civil Secretary Reply to President of Congress (29th April, 1942).

Congress Memorandum to Governor-General (12th May, 1942).

Civil Secretary's letter to President of Congress (16th June, 1942).

Civil Secretary's letter to President of Congress (17th July, 1942).

Letter from President of Congress to Sir Douglas Newbold (Civil Secretary) (23th July, 1942).

Proceedings of the Advisory Council for the Northern Sudan 1944–1947.

Executive Council and Legislative Assembly Ordinance 1948.

Weekly Digest of the Proceedings of the first Legislative Assembly 1948–1950.

M. A. Mahgoub and A. Khalil to President of the Security Council enclosing a note titled 'A Case for Independent Sudan' dated August 22nd, 1947.

Verbatim Records of the discussions of the 175th, 176th, 179th, 182nd, 189th, 193rd 200th, and 201st Meetings of the Security Council, (August–September, 1947).

Constitution and Regulations of the Umma Party, 1945.

Note on the Ashigga Party (MS) by the Secretary of the Ashigga Party (1947).

Constitution of the Ittihadiyn Party (MS) 1947.

Notes by Presidents of the Unity of the Nile Valley and Gawmiyn Parties (MS) (1947

General Policy of the Republican Party (1945).

Report of the Nile Projects Commission, Cairo, 1920.

B SECONDARY AUTHORITIES CONSULTED

ABBAS HILMI, II Khedive of Egypt, *A Few words on the Anglo-Egyptian Settlement*, London, 1930.

ABDEL KAWI AHMED, *The Nile Link between Egypt and the Sudan* (Arabic) (*The Engineers Magazine*), Cairo, May, 1948.

AHMED KHAIR, *The Struggle of a Generation* (Arabic), Cairo, 1948.

ALLEN, B. M., *Gordon and the Sudan*, London, 1931.

ANTONIUS, G., *The Arab Awakening*, London, 1938.

ARKELL, A. J., *An Outline History of the Sudan*, Khartoum, 1945.

ATIYAH, E., *An Arab Tells His Story*, London, 1946.

AUSTRALIAN DEPARTMENT OF EXTERNAL AFFAIRS, *Anglo-Egyptian Sudan*, in *Current Notes on International Affairs*, Vol. 20, Canberra 1949.

AWAD, DR. M., *The River Nile*, Cairo, 1937.

BAKER, Sir Samuel, *The Albert Nyanza*, London, 1866. *Ismailia*, London, 1879.

BOARD OF TRADE, *Egypt, Economic and Commercial Conditions*, London, 1948.

BONNE, A., *The Economic Development of the Middle East*, London, 1945.
State and Economics in the Middle East, London, 1948.

BRIERLEY, J. L., *The Law of Nations*, Oxford, 1942.

BROWNE, W. G., *Travels in Africa, Egypt and Syria*, London, 1799.

BRUCE, James, *Travels to discover the Sources of the Nile*, Edinburgh, 1813.

BUDGE, E. A. Wallis, *The Egyptian Sudan*, its history and monuments, London, 1907.

BURCKHARDT, J. L., *Travels in Nubia*, London, 1891.

BUXTON, T. F., *The African Slave Trade and its Remedy*, London, 1840.

CHAMBERLAIN, J., *Foreign and Colonial Speeches*, London, 1897.

COLVIN, Sir Auckland, *The Making of Modern Egypt*, London, 1906.

COUPLAND, R., *The British Anti-Slavery Movement*, Oxford, 1933.

CRABITÈS, Pierre, *Egypt, the Sudan and the Nile*, Foreign Affairs, Vol. 3, New York, 1924.
The Winning of the Sudan, London, 1934.
The Nile Waters Agreement, Foreign Affairs, Vol. 8, New York, 1929.

CROMER, Earl of, *Ancient and Modern Imperialism*, London, 1901.
Modern Egypt, 2 Vols., London, 1908.
Abbas II, London, 1915.

CURRIE, Sir James, *The Educational Experiment in the Anglo-Egyptian Sudan*, (*Journal of the African Society* Vols. 33 and 34), London, 1933 and 1934.

DE LA WARR, Lord, *Report of Educational Commission, 1937*, Khartoum, 1937.

EGYPTIAN GOVERNMENT, *Annuaire Statistique*, Cairo, 1948.

ELGOOD, P. G., *The Transit of Egypt*, London, 1928.

EVANS-PRITCHARD, E. E., *The Nuer*, Oxford, 1940.

FABIAN COLONIAL BUREAU, *The Sudan: The Road Ahead*, London, 1945.

FABIAN SOCIETY, *Fabian Colonial Essays*, London, 1945.

FULLER, F. W., *Egypt and the Hinterland to the re-opening of the Sudan*, London, 1903.

GARSTIN, Sir William, *The Basin of the Upper Nile*, London, 1904.

GHORBAL, DR. M. S., *The Building up of a single Egyptian Sudanese Fatherland*, (*The Unity of the Nile Valley—Its Geographical Bases and Manifestations in History*), Cairo, 1947.

GIFFORD, G., *The Sudan at War* (*Journal of the Royal African Society* Vol. 42), London, 1943.

GILLAN, Sir Angus, *The Sudan: past, present and future*, (*African Affairs* Vol. 43), London, 1944.

GORMAN, J. P., *The Laws of the Sudan*, Khartoum, 1941.

HAMILTON, J. A. DE C., *Anglo-Egyptian Sudan From Within*, London, 1935.

HENDERSON, K. D. D., *The Sudan and the Abyssinian Campaign* (*Journal of the Royal African Society*, Vol. 42), London 1943.

HILL, R., *A Bibliography of the Anglo-Egyptian Sudan to 1937*, Oxford, 1939.

HERTZLET, Sir Edward, *The Map of Africa by Treaty*, London, 1909.

HURST, H. E., *Major Irrigation Projects on the Nile* (*Civil Engineering and Public Works Review*, Vol. 43, No. 507), London, 1948.

HIRST, H. E., BLACK, R. P., AND SIMAIKA, Y., *The Future Conservation of the Nile*, Cairo, 1946.

ISSAWI, C., *Egypt: an Economic and Social Analysis*, London, 1947.

JACKSON, Sir Herbert W., *Fashoda, 1898* (*Sudan Notes and Records*, Vol. 3), Cairo, 1920.

KLINGBERG, F. J., *The Anti-Slavery movement in England*, New Haven, 1926.

LANGER, W. L., *The Diplomacy of Imperialism*, 2 Vols., New York, 1935.
    The Struggle for the Nile (*Foreign Affairs*, Vol. 14), New York, 1936.

LAUTERBACHT, H., *Oppenheim's International Law*, Vol. 1, London, 1947.

LAWERENCE, T. J., *The Principles of International Law*, London, 1947.

LLOYD, Lord, *Egypt Since Cromer*, 2 Vols., London, 1933.

LOGAN, R. W., *The Anglo-Egyptian Sudan, a problem in international relations* (*Journal of Negro History*, Vol. 16), Lancaster, 1931.

MACDONALD, Sir Murdoch, *Nile Control*, Cairo, 1920.

MACMICHAEL, Sir Harold A., *A History of the Arabs in the Sudan*, 2 Vols., Cambridge, 1922.
    The Anglo-Egyptian Sudan, London, 1934.

MARSHALL, A. H., *Report on Local Government in the Sudan*, Khartoum, 1949.

MILNER, Lord, *England in Egypt*, London, 1903.

MINISTRY OF INFORMATION, *The Abyssinian Campaigns*, London, 1942.

MOON, P. T., *Imperialism and World Politics*, New York, 1927.

MUIR, R., *A Short History of the British Commonwealth*, 2 Vols., London, 1949.

MURRAY, T. D. and WHITE, A. S., *Sir Samuel Baker, A Memoir*, London, 1895.

NATIONAL BANK OF EGYPT, 1898–1948, Cairo, 1949.

NEWBOLD, Sir Douglas, *The Share of the Sudanese in the Government of the Sudan* (Bulletin of Uganda Society, No. 3), Kampala, 1944.

O'ROURKE, V. A., *The British Position in Egypt*, (Foreign Affairs, Vol. 14), New York, 1936.
    The Juristic Status of Egypt and the Sudan, (*The John Hopkins University Studies in Historical and Political Science*, Series 53), Baltimore, 1935.

OSMAN, Y. and MAHGOUB, M. A., *The Sudan for Liberty*, (*Pan Africa*, Vol. 1, No. 3), Manchester, 1947.

PERHAM, Margery F., *The Sudan Emerges into Nationhood*, (*Foreign Affairs*, Vol. 27), New York, 1947.

PERHAM, M. F. and SIMMONS, J., *African Discovery*, London, 1942.

RAFII, Abdel Rahman El, *Mustafa Kemal*, Cairo, 1945.
    Mohammed Fareed, Cairo, 1948.
    The Arabi Revolution, Cairo, 1937.
    Following the Egyptian Revolution, Cairo, 1947.
    The 1919 Revolution, 2 Vols., Cairo, 1946.
    History of the Nationalist Movement in Egypt, 2 Vols., Cairo, 1948.
    Egypt and the Sudan, 1882–1892, Cairo, 1948.
    The Era of Mohammed Ali, Cairo, 1947.

ROBINSON, A. E., *The Conquest of the Sudan by the Wali of Egypt*, I, II (*Journal of the African Society*, Vol. 25), London, 1925.

ROYAL INSTITUTE OF INTERNATIONAL AFFAIRS, *Egypt and Great Britain, 1914–1936*, London, 1936.
    The Political and Strategic Interests of the United Kingdom, Oxford, 1940.
    The Middle East, London, 1950.

SHOUCAIR, N., *The History and Geography of the Sudan*, 3 Vols., Cairo, 1903.

SHUKRY, M. F., *Egypt and Sovereignty over the Sudan*, (Arabic), Cairo, 1946.

SIMAIKA, Y., *The Unity of the Nile Valley from the Hydrological point of View* (*The Engineers Magazine*), Cairo, May, 1948.

SIMPSON, M. F., *Report of a Commission of Inspection on the Gordon Memorial College, Khartoum*, London, 1929.

SMITH, H. A., *The Economic uses of International Rivers*, London, 1931.

SUDAN GOVERNMENT, *The Sudan: Record of Progress 1898-1947*, Khartoum, 1947.
    The Sudan: Review of Commercial Conditions, London, 1947.

SYMES, Sir George Stewart, *Tour of Duty*, London, 1946.

TAHA HUSSEIN, *The Future of Culture in Egypt*, Cairo, 1938.

TAYLOR, A. J. P., *Prelude to Fashoda, the question of the Upper Nile 1894–5*, (*English Historical Review*, Vol. 65), London, 1950.

TOTHILL, J. D., *Agriculture in the Sudan*, Oxford, 1948.

TOYNBEE, A. J., *Survey of International Affairs, 1925*, Vol. 1, Oxford, 1927.

TRIMINGHAM, J. S., *The Christian Approach to Islam in the Sudan*, Oxford, 1948.

UMAR TUSSIN, Prince, *Memorandum on the question of Sudan*, Alexandria, 1936.

WARD, A. W., and GOOCH, G. P., *Cambridge History of British Foreign Policy*, Vol. III Cambridge, 1923.

WARRINER, Doreen, *Land and Poverty in the Middle East*, London, 1948.

WAVELL, Lord, *Allenby in Egypt*, London, 1944.

WHITE, A. S., *The Expansion of Egypt*, London, 1899

WIGHT, M., *The Development of the Legislative Council, 1606–1945*, London, 1945.

WINGATE, F. R., *Mahdiism and the Egyptian Sudan*, London, 1891.

WINTER, R. K., *Education in the Northern Sudan*, Report of a Committee appointed by the Governor-General, 1933, Khartoum, 1934.

INDEX

Index

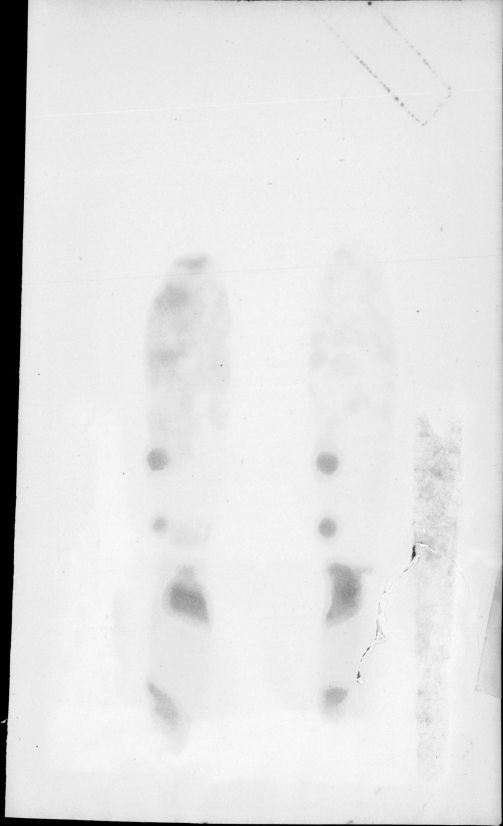

12/15/52

DATE DUE	

SUBSTANCE ABUSE ON CAMPUS